Scalable Architecture Basics

Velabhai Bhedaru

Introduction

The purpose of this book is to understand the backend scalability and things to consider while handling large volume of traffic.
If you have further questions, contact Velabhai Bhedaru. Our regular business hours are Mon-Thurs. 8:30 am to 8 pm PST, and Friday 8:30 am to 5 pm. During these hours, you can reach us by phone, email or on-line chat. Outside of these hours, either call and leave a message or email us.
Phone: 4085123344
Email: vbbhedaru@gmail.com

Table of Contents

Architecture

In today's realm, we collect data either from user or from IOT devices and store it on the backend for retrieval when needed. The back-end design should be scalable to handle large volume of data coming from the field. The server capacity depends on how much data transferred in I/O operation. Singe instance can handle certain amount of data based on CPU and memory resources. To handle large volume of traffic, load balancer or proxy server is used to distribute the load. NGINX server is very popular in selecting the load balancer.

There are many open source back-end platforms available to handle low level communication and to keep developer focused on the business logic, many company prefers to use out of the box open source solution like Spring MVC framework. This platform is very matured and community has developed many plugins to support more protocols and concept. We will discuss in details in the next chapter.

The database selection depends on type of business requirements. There 2 types of database: relational (RDBMS-Relational database management system) and non-relational(NO-SQL). The relational database has references in built and record can be searched though nested query. The record should be indexed with keys for fast look up and table schema are normalized. My-SQL, Oracle database falls into this RDBMS category. In case of Non- relational database, everything is stored as key value pair for fast retrieval, there are no join operation between tables. This database stores object as key value pair. Care should be taken to make sure keys are equally distributed among multiple nodes. For example, there should be separate key for each user and if possible for each device. For example, select UUID as user Id or device Id to ensure request from each user or device can be distributed among nodes.

There are options to self-manage the database or use as services option. In the database as service option, we don't have to deal with hardware or configuration management. Where in case of self-manage database, we need database administer (DBA) to configure and manage the hardware. To focus on the business logic many organizations select database as service option. This is preferred approach to improve time to market the solution.

The configuration and static data are often cached in instance memory to optimize the database calls. This cached data can be stored as in-memory instance or on separate node shared by multiple instances. Redis and Memcahe are very popular cache engines developed to handle this kind of data and discussed later in this book.

There is also a case when event is produced and consumed at different speed. Message Queue is used to hold and forward the data. RabbitMQ and Kafaka is open source message broker designed for these categories of design.

Spring Basics

Spring is the most popular application development framework for enterprise Java and it allows to create high performing, easily testable, reusable code.

Spring framework is an open source Java platform and it was initially written by Rod Johnson and was first released under the Apache 2.0 license in June 2003.

Spring is lightweight when it comes to size and transparency. The basic version of spring framework is around 2MB.

The core features of the Spring Framework can be used in developing any Java application, but there are extensions for building web applications on top of the Java EE platform. Spring framework targets to make J2EE development easier to use and promote good programming practice by enabling a POJO-based programming model.

Dependency Injection (DI)

The technology that Spring is most identified with is the Dependency Injection (DI) flavor of Inversion of Control. The Inversion of Control (IoC) is a general concept, and it can be expressed in many different ways and Dependency Injection is merely one concrete example of Inversion of Control.

When writing a complex Java application, application classes should be as independent as possible of other Java classes to increase the possibility to reuse these classes and to test them independently of other classes while doing unit testing. Dependency Injection helps in gluing these classes together and same time keeping them independent.

What is dependency injection exactly? Let's look at these two words separately. Here the dependency part translates into an association between two classes. For example, class A is dependent on class B. Now, let's look at the second part, injection. All this means is that class B will get injected into class A by the IoC.

Dependency injection can happen in the way of passing parameters to the constructor or by post-construction using setter methods.

In this sample example BlueColor class is injected through auto wire.

```
public interface MyColor {
   public void printColor();
}

public class BlueColor implements MyColor {
   @Override
   public void printColor() {
      System.out.println("It is blue in color...");
   }
}

@Service
public class ColorManager {
   private MyColor color;
    /**
    * dependency injection through autowire
    * @param myColor
    */
   @Autowired
   public void setMyColor(MyColor myColor){
      this.color = myColor;
   }
   public void printColor(){
      this.color.printColor();
   }

}
```

pom.xml

```
<beans xmlns="http://www.springframework.org/schema/beans"
   xmlns:xsi="http://www.w3.org/2001/XMLSchema-instance"
   xsi:schemaLocation="http://www.springframework.org/schema/beans
   http://www.springframework.org/schema/beans/spring-beans-3.0.xsd">
<bean id="colorManager" class="com.company.bean.ColorManager">
      <property name="myColor" ref="blueColor" />
</bean>
```

```
<bean id="blueColor" class="BlueColor" />
</beans>
```

Aspect Oriented Programming (AOP)

One of the key components of Spring is the Aspect oriented programming (AOP) framework. The functions that span multiple points of an application are called cross-cutting concerns and these cross-cutting concerns are conceptually separate from the application's business logic. There are various common good examples of aspects including logging, declarative transactions, security, and caching etc.

The key unit of modularity in OOP is the class, whereas in AOP the unit of modularity is the aspect. Whereas DI helps you decouple your application objects from each other, AOP helps you decouple cross-cutting concerns from the objects that they affect.

The AOP module of Spring Framework provides aspect-oriented programming implementation allowing you to define method-interceptors and point cuts to cleanly decouple code that implements functionality that should be separated.
There are 4 types of advices supported in spring1.2 old style aop implementation.

Before Advice: it is executed before the actual method call.
After Advice: it is executed after the actual method call. If method returns a value, it is executed after returning value.
Around Advice: it is executed before and after the actual method call.
Throws Advice: it is executed if actual method throws exception.

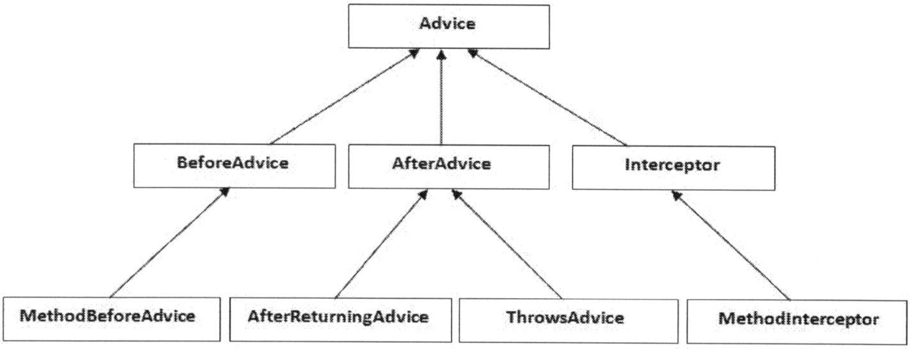

It is explained here with three steps:

Step1: Define AOP interface

```
@Target(ElementType.METHOD)
@Retention(RetentionPolicy.RUNTIME)
public @interface AddEventForAction {
}
```

Step 2: Implement AOP intercepter

```
@Aspect
public class ActionHandlingAspect {


        @Pointcut(value =
        "@annotation(com.company.aop.AddEventForAction) " +
            "&& args(foo, abc,..,session)", argNames = "foo, abc,
        session")
          public void updateMethodA(Foo foo, String abc, HttpSession
        session) {
          }

        @Before(value = "updateMotionTime(motionAlert, abc, session)",
        argNames = "motionAlert, abc, session")
          public void updateMethodBeforeA(Foo foo, String abc,
        HttpSession session) {
                executeAOPAction(foo, session, abc);
          }

          private void executeAOPAction(
            Foo foo,
            HttpSession session,
            String abc
          ){
           //Add code to be executed through AOP
          }
}
```

Step 3: Class that invokes AOP method

```
@Controller
@EnableAspectJAutoProxy
@RequestMapping("/user")
public class SampleController {
```

```
        @AddEventForAction
        @RequestMapping( value= "/action",   method =
RequestMethod.POST)
        public ResponseEntity<Resource> doprocess(
                @Valid @RequestBody Foo foo,
                @RequestHeader("abc") String abc,
                HttpServletRequest request,
                HttpSession session
        ){
         //code to execute after AOP AddEventForAction is executed
        }
}
```

Spring - IoC Containers

The Spring container is at the core of the Spring Framework. The container will create the objects, wire them together, configure them, and manage their complete lifecycle from creation till destruction. The Spring container uses dependency injection (DI) to manage the components that make up an application. These objects are called Spring Beans.

The container gets its instructions on what objects to instantiate, configure, and assemble by reading configuration metadata provided. The configuration metadata can be represented either by XML, Java annotations, or Java code. The following diagram is a high-level view of how Spring works. The Spring IoC container makes use of Java POJO classes and configuration metadata to produce a fully configured and executable system or application.

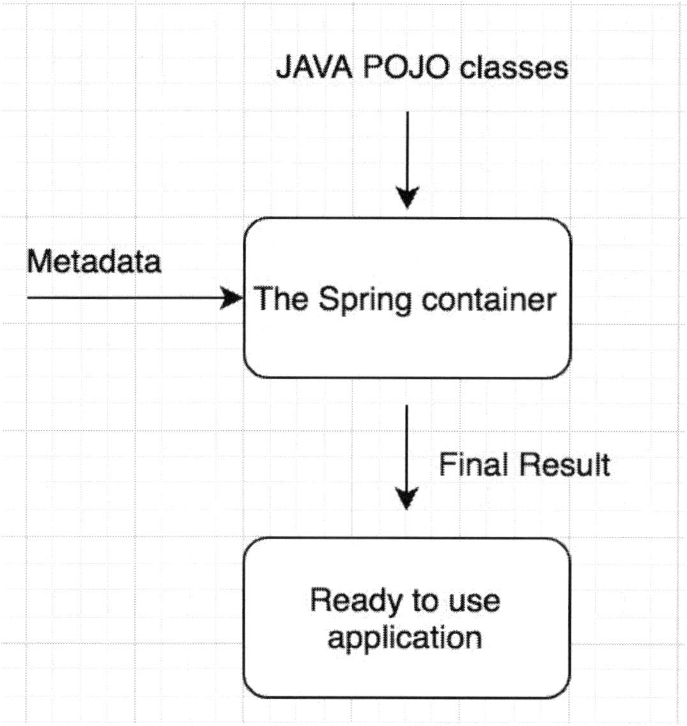

The objects that form the backbone of your application and that are managed by the Spring IoC container are called beans. A bean is an object that is instantiated, assembled, and otherwise managed by a Spring IoC container.

When defining a <bean> in Spring, you have the option of declaring a scope for that bean. For example, to force Spring to produce a new bean instance each time one is needed, you should declare the bean's scope attribute to be prototype. Similar way if you want Spring to return the same bean instance each time one is needed, you should declare the bean's scope attribute to be singleton.

Spring Bean scopes

Singleton- This scope the bean definition to a single instance per Spring IoC container (default).
Prototype- This scope a single bean definition to have any number of object instances.

Request- This scope a bean definition to an HTTP request. Only valid in the context of a web-aware Spring Application Context.
Session- This scope a bean definition to an HTTP session. Only valid in the context of a web-aware Spring Application Context.
global-session- This scope a bean definition to a global HTTP session. Only valid in the context of a web-aware Spring Application Context.

The Spring web MVC framework provides model-view-controller architecture and ready components that can be used to develop flexible and loosely coupled web applications. The MVC pattern results in separating the different aspects of the application (input logic, business logic, and UI logic), while providing a loose coupling between these elements.

The Model encapsulates the application data and in general they will consist of POJO.

The View is responsible for rendering the model data and in general it generates HTML output that the client's browser can interpret.

The Controller is responsible for processing user requests and building appropriate model and passes it to the view for rendering.

Stateless Bean:

```
Service
public class Calculator {
  public int sum(int a, int b) {
      return a + b;
  }

}
```

When two "requests" invoke sum method of the bean at the same time, that would mean the sum method would be executed concurrently in two different threads. Hence, they will have their own execution context which won't overlap with each other. This would safely allow them to run concurrently.

Bean which share class variable in singleton scope:

```
@Service
public class Calculator {
  int incrementalMultiplier = 0;
  public int mulitply(int a, int b) {
```

```
        incrementalMultiplier++;
        return a * b * incrementalMultiplier;
    }
}
```

This could cause issues when serving two requests concurrently because the incrementalMultiplier is the object level state that will be shared by the two requests (threads) and hence could produce unexpected results.
A stateless singleton will be able to serve two requests concurrently because they will be in different threads. Each API call to container creates new thread.

The Dispatcher Servlet

The Spring Web model-view-controller (MVC) framework is designed around a Dispatcher Servlet that handles all the HTTP requests and responses.

The request processing workflow of the Spring Web MVC Dispatcher Servlet is illustrated in the following diagram:

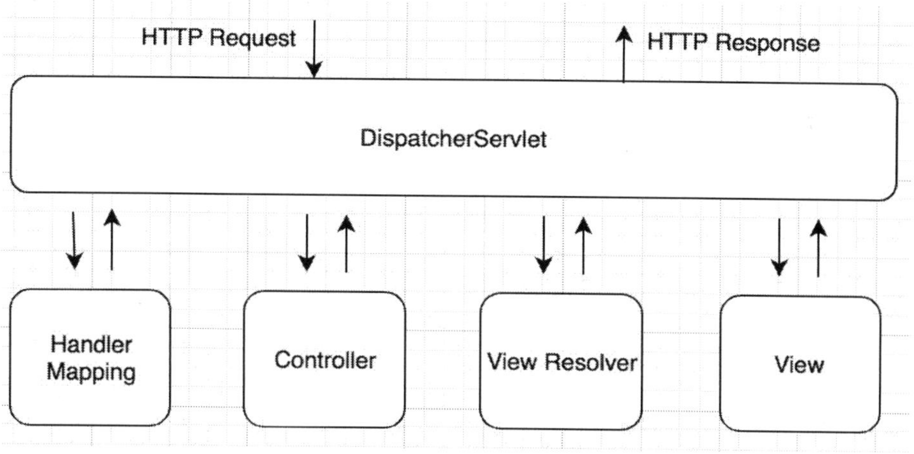

Following is the sequence of events corresponding to an incoming HTTP request to Dispatcher Servlet:

After receiving an HTTP request, Dispatcher Servlet consults the Handler Mapping to call the appropriate Controller.

The Controller takes the request and calls the appropriate service methods based on used GET or POST method. The service method will set model data based on defined business logic and returns view name to the Dispatcher Servlet.

The Dispatcher Servlet will take help from View Resolver to pick up the defined view for the request.

Once view is finalized, The Dispatcher Servlet passes the model data to the view which is finally rendered on the browser.

All the above-mentioned components i.e. Handler Mapping, Controller and View Resolver are parts of Web Application Context which is an extension of the plain Application Context with some extra features necessary for web applications.

Configuration Class:

```
@Configuration
@Import({ ServicesConfiguration.class})
@ComponentScan("com.companyname.modulename")
@EnableWebMvc
public class MvcConfiguration extends WebMvcConfigurerAdapter {

	@Bean
	public ViewResolver getViewResolver() {
	InternalResourceViewResolver resolver = new
InternalResourceViewResolver();
		resolver.setPrefix("/");
		resolver.setSuffix(".html");
		return resolver;
	}


}
```

Web Application Configuration:

Web.xml:

```
<?xml version="1.0" encoding="UTF-8"?>
<!DOCTYPE xml>
<web-app version="3.0" xmlns="http://java.sun.com/xml/ns/j2ee"
```

```
        xmlns:xsi="http://www.w3.org/2001/XMLSchema-instance"
        xsi:schemaLocation="http://java.sun.com/xml/ns/javaee
http://java.sun.com/xml/ns/javaee/web-app_3_0.xsd">

<display-name>Name Of the Application</display-name>

<!-- Configure ContextLoaderListener to use
AnnotationConfigWebApplicationContext instead of the default
XmlWebApplicationContext -->
 <context-param>
    <param-name>contextClass</param-name>
    <param-value>
        org.springframework.web.context.support.AnnotationConfigWebA
pplicationContext
     </param-value>
  </context-param>
  <context-param>
    <param-name>contextConfigLocation</param-name>
    <param-value>com.companyname.config.MvcConfiguration
    </param-value>
  </context-param>
  <listener>
    <listener-class>
        org.springframework.web.context.ContextLoaderListener
    </listener-class>
  </listener>

<servlet>
        <servlet-name>SpringDispatcher</servlet-name>
        <servlet-class>
                org.springframework.web.servlet.DispatcherServlet
        </servlet-class>
        <init-param>
                <param-name>contextConfigLocation</param-name>
                 <param-value></param-value>
        </init-param>
   <!-- delegate options handling to Controller -->
        <init-param>
                <param-name>dispatchOptionsRequest</param-name>
                <param-value>true</param-value>
        </init-param>
        <load-on-startup>1</load-on-startup>
```

```
        <async-supported>true</async-supported>
        </servlet>
        <servlet-mapping>
                <servlet-name>SpringDispatcher</servlet-name>
                <url-pattern>/</url-pattern>
        </servlet-mapping>

        <servlet-mapping>
                <servlet-name>default</servlet-name>
                <url-pattern>*.html</url-pattern>
        </servlet-mapping>
        <servlet-mapping>
                <servlet-name>default</servlet-name>
                <url-pattern>*.css</url-pattern>
        </servlet-mapping>
        <servlet-mapping>
                <servlet-name>default</servlet-name>
                <url-pattern>*.js</url-pattern>
        </servlet-mapping>
        <servlet-mapping>
                <servlet-name>default</servlet-name>
                <url-pattern>*.png</url-pattern>
        </servlet-mapping>
        <servlet-mapping>
                <servlet-name>default</servlet-name>
                <url-pattern>*.swf</url-pattern>
        </servlet-mapping>
        <servlet-mapping>
                <servlet-name>default</servlet-name>
                <url-pattern>*.json</url-pattern>
        </servlet-mapping>
        <session-config>
                <session-timeout>30</session-timeout>
                <cookie-config>
        <path>/</path>
      </cookie-config>
        </session-config>
        <welcome-file-list>
                <welcome-file>index.html</welcome-file>
        </welcome-file-list>
</web-app>
```

Spring – Deferred Result

Asynchronous support introduced in Servlet 3.0 offers the possibility to process an HTTP request in another thread. This is especially important when you have a long running task, since while another thread processes this request, the container thread is freed and can continue serving other requests.

Here is example how response is managed by application thread using Spring's Differed Result and container thread is free. This is preferred to handle transactional request handling where the response of this API call depend on outcome from another thread.

```
@RestController
public class AsyncDeferredController {
  private final Logger logger = LoggerFactory.getLogger(this.getClass());
  private final TaskService taskService;

  @Autowired
  public AsyncDeferredController(TaskService taskService) {
    this.taskService = taskService;
  }

  @RequestMapping(value = "/deferred", method = RequestMethod.GET,
produces = "text/html")
  public DeferredResult<String> executeSlowTask() {

    logger.info("Request received");
    DeferredResult<String> deferredResult = new DeferredResult<>();
    CompletableFuture.supplyAsync(taskService::execute)
      .whenCompleteAsync((result, throwable) ->
deferredResult.setResult(result));
    logger.info("Servlet thread released");

    return deferredResult;
  }
}
```

We can also return default error value incase if thread exceed timeout values:

```
deferredResult.onTimeout(()-> {
        deferredResult.setErrorResult(
            new ResponseEntity<>(new Resource<>( Default error
values()), HttpStatus.OK));
});
```

Spring - Mail Sender

Spring comes with utility libraries which abstracts away the complexities of the underlying mailing system, provides super-simple API to use in application to send emails.

The email support in spring is built upon Java Mail API which must be found on class path. In below example, javax.mail is included in pom.xml.

Configuration in POM.xml

```
<dependency>
        <groupId>javax.mail</groupId>
        <artifactId>mail</artifactId>
        <version>1.4.7</version>
</dependency>
```

Java Bean initialization:

```
@Bean
public JavaMailSender mailSender() {

        JavaMailSenderImpl mailSender = new JavaMailSenderImpl();
        mailSender.setHost(IPropertiesConstant.SMTP_HOST);
        mailSender.setPort(new
        Integer(IPropertiesConstant.SMTP_PORT));
        mailSender.setUsername(IPropertiesConstant.SMTP_USER_NA
        ME);
        mailSender.setPassword(IPropertiesConstant.SMTP_PASSWORD
        );
        Properties javaMailProperties = new Properties();
        javaMailProperties.put("mail.smtp.from",
        IPropertiesConstant.SMTP_FROM);
        mailSender.setJavaMailProperties(javaMailProperties);
        mailSender.setDefaultEncoding("UTF-8");
        return mailSender;
}

try {
   MimeMessage message = createParamsForEmail();
   mailSender.send(message);
```

```
   }
catch (MailSendException mse) {
 }

private MimeMessage createParamsForEmail() throws
MessagingException {
        MimeMessage message = this.mailSender.createMimeMessage();
        MimeMessageHelper helper;
        helper = new MimeMessageHelper(message, true, "UTF-8");
        String[] emailIdArray = this.emailIdList.toArray(new
String[this.emailIdList.size()]);

        helper.setTo(emailIdArray);
        helper.setSubject(subject);
        helper.setText(emailBody, true);
        return message;
}
```

Spring – Velocity Template

Java has inbuilt support to send email. Apache Velocity is a Java-based template engine that provides a template language to reference objects defined in Java code. It aims to ensure clean separation between the presentation tier and business tiers in a Web application (the model–view–controller design pattern).

As of Spring 4.3.x, Velocity templates are deprecated, and Freemarker is the preferred choice to go for.

```
/*
    * FreeMarker configuration.
    */
   @Bean
   public FreeMarkerConfigurationFactoryBean
getFreeMarkerConfiguration() {
      FreeMarkerConfigurationFactoryBean bean = new
FreeMarkerConfigurationFactoryBean();
      bean.setTemplateLoaderPath("/fmtemplates/");
      return bean;
   }

   /*
    * Velocity configuration.
    */


@Bean
public VelocityEngine velocity() throws VelocityException, IOException {
        VelocityEngineFactory factory = new VelocityEngineFactory();
        factory.setPreferFileSystemAccess(false);
        factory.setResourceLoaderPath("/emailtemplates");

        Properties properties = new Properties();
        properties.setProperty("string.resource.loader.description","Velocit
y StringResource loader");
        properties.setProperty("string.resource.loader.class","org.apache.v
elocity.runtime.resource.loader.StringResourceLoader");
        properties.setProperty("string.resource.loader.repository.class","or
g.apache.velocity.runtime.resource.util.StringResourceRepositoryImpl");
```

```
        properties.setProperty("string.resource.loader.repository.name","re
po");
        properties.setProperty("resource.loader","string");
        properties.setProperty("input.encoding","UTF-8");
        properties.setProperty("output.encoding","UTF-8");
        properties.setProperty(RuntimeConstants.RUNTIME_LOG_LOG
SYSTEM_CLASS,"org.apache.velocity.runtime.log.Log4JLogChute");
        factory.setVelocityProperties(properties);

        return factory.createVelocityEngine();
}

//Sample code where parameter substitution is wired.
private String createMessageBody(EmailTemplate emailTemplateObj,
Map<String, Object> data) {
        String emailBody = null;
        try {
        StringResourceRepository repo =
StringResourceLoader.getRepository("repo");
        String myTemplateName = emailTemplateObj.getName();
        String myTemplate = emailTemplateObj.getContent();
        repo.putStringResource(myTemplateName, myTemplate);
        data.put("locale", LocaleContextHolder.getLocale());

        emailBody =
VelocityEngineUtils.mergeTemplateIntoString(this.velocityEngine,
myTemplateName, "UTF-8", data);


        } catch (ResourceNotFoundException e) {
        } catch (Exception e) {
                e.printStackTrace();
        }

        return emailBody;
}
```

Http Client

Apache Http client library is very popular in handling communication with external services. Apache 4.3 has support to tune connection pool and customize SSL support.

```
@Bean
public HttpClient ApacheInternalHttpClient(ApiClientConfig
clientConfig) {
        int connectionTimeout = clientConfig.getRequestTimeoutMillis();
        RequestConfig requestConfig = RequestConfig.custom()
                .setConnectTimeout(connectionTimeout)
                .setConnectionRequestTimeout(connectionTimeout)
                .setSocketTimeout(connectionTimeout)
                .build();

                PoolingHttpClientConnectionManager connectionManager
        = new PoolingHttpClientConnectionManager();
        connectionManager.setDefaultMaxPerRoute(clientConfig.getMax
PoolSize());

        httpClient = HttpClientBuilder.create()
                .setDefaultRequestConfig(requestConfig)
                .setConnectionManager(connectionManager)
                .build();
        return httpClient;
}
```

Caching Data

Caching is a technique that enables applications or devices store data that is likely to be reused in memory, so that the data may be served faster in subsequent requests. The data can be read from database, web pages, etc. By adding caches to your servers, you can avoid reading or creating the same data record from database or web pages, thus reduce both the response time and the load on your server. Consequently, your application becomes more scalable.

The data is cached when it is shared across multiple processes, multiple applications or multiple servers or to communicate with cross-platform. This is some time cost effective solution than storing in to the database. There are many platforms support highly scalable caching data. Radis and Mem cache are very popular engine designed to support cache.

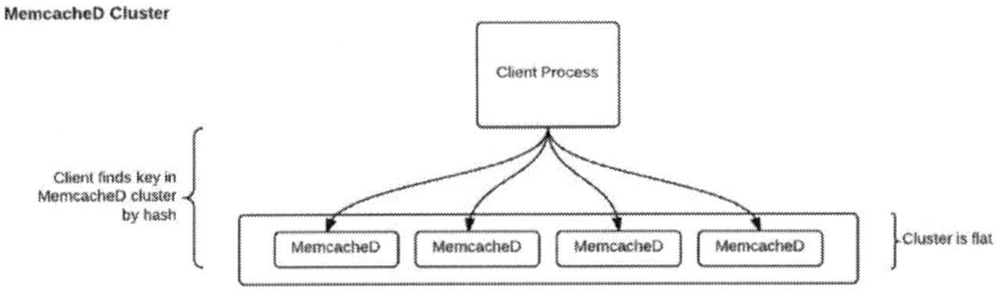

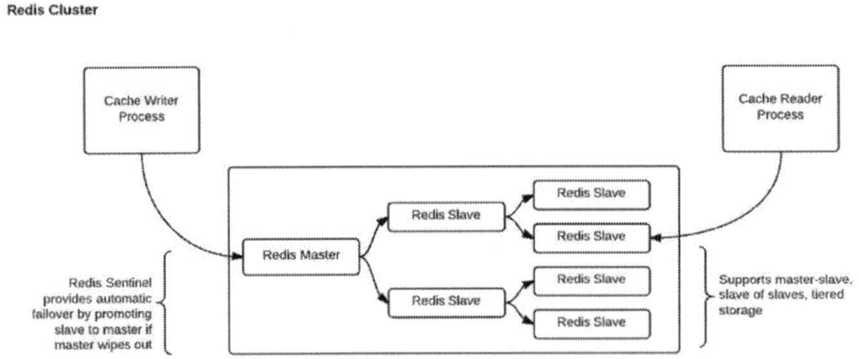

Memcached has a flat architecture while Redis uses Master-Slave and Slave of Slaves.

Redis

Redis is more than a key/value store. It is an in-memory data structure server. Keys can be assigned simple strings, like in memcached, but they can also store Hashes, Lists, Sets, or Sorted Sets.
Redis offers persistence, built-in and on by default. This means redis is a real database by default, and not a simple volatile cache like memcached. Your data will be there when you restart.
Redis offers Publish/Subscribe. This allows you to create channels and have one or more clients subscribe to them, allowing an efficient high-speed real-time communication mechanism. This can be a great solution for inter-process, inter-application, or inter-server communication.
Redis offers Lua scripting support. This allows you to do all sorts of new things. One important example would be executing several dependent redis commands atomically, and with a single call to redis. Lua scripting is easy to pick up and the scripts run efficiently and atomically.

There are pro and cons of using Redis in Master/slave and clustered configuration.

Dis-advantage of Master/Slave configuration:
1. There will be only one Master with multiple slaves for replication.
2. All write goes to Master, which creates more load on master node.
3. If Master goes down, whole architecture is prone to SPOF (Single point of failure).
4. M-S architecture does not help in scaling, when your user base grows. So we need a process to Monitor Master in case of failure or shutdown, that is Sentinel. We need to run Sentinel on each server, and also we need separate process to monitor sentinel, to restart in case if sentinel is down. Basically we use Sentinel, to do fail-over when Master is down. i.e. promote any of the slave as a Master. But in some scenarios Sentinel fails to do the fail-over.
5. Sentinel cannot start fail-over without an authorization from majority of sentinels.
6. If slaves were restarted and never was connected to Master after the restart, data replication to that slave is skipped causing byzantine failure.

Redis Cluster is a distributed implementation of Redis with the following goals:
High performance and linear scalability up to 1000 nodes
Acceptable degree of write safety
Availability

The demerit of cluster architecture:
Requires at least 3 Masters with 2 slaves each to setup architecture.
Since Data is sharded based on the hash-slots assigned to each Master. If Master holding some slots is down, data to be written to that slot will be lost.
Clients connecting to Redis cluster should be aware of the cluster topology, causing overhead configuration on Clients.
Failover does not happen unless master have at least one slave.
Slave promotion as a Master takes at least 30–50 seconds, so data written to cluster in that time window will be lost.

Memcached

Memcached is a “high-performance, distributed memory object caching system, generic in nature, but intended for use in speeding up dynamic web applications by alleviating database load.” (From http://memcached.org) Memcached caches data, objects and database query results in RAM (hence the name “memory caching”) for fast retrieval of data by utilizing key value stores. It is a distributed memory cache solution and can leverages memory of multiple servers by virtualizing them together. Each individual server node is responsible for its own memory allocated for caching and does not need to be aware of memory allocations on other servers. The servers’ memory spaces form a single logical memory, accessible by application servers. Using this attribute, memcached can easily be scaled horizontally by adding more servers to the server pool.

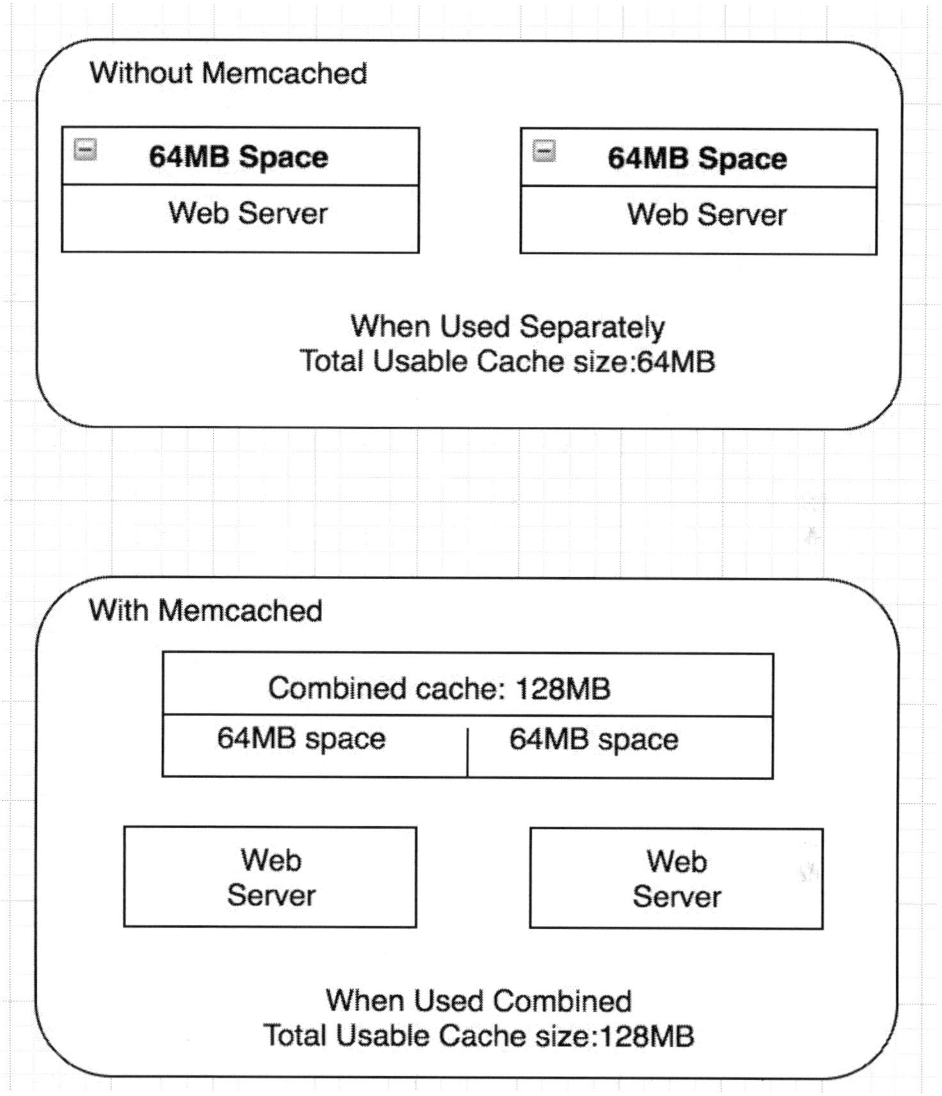

Memcached works by virtualizing the memory of different servers into one big logical memory space. (Credit: http://memcached.org/) This distributed solution counteracts problems such as memory space constraints. Without distributed caching, each server will operate separate cache spaces which may result in redundancy if they cache the same data. A typical size for the memory is 4GB for 32-bit systems. However, by combining memory space of multiple servers, Memcached can create a memory cache space of the 100GB or more

Source:
http://memcached.org/about

Memcached Pros:
Low complexity
Simple to configure
Few command macros == simple to master
Atomic increment and decrement
Simple to cluster -- uses a hashing algorithm at the client to find keys in a cluster
Can withstand a member dying
Many years in production
Every programming language has a memcached library.

Memcached Cons:
Doesn't do anything besides be an in-memory key/value store
Caches sharded by client do not scale across AWS zones
Unbalanced memcached clusters require a full system restart
Adding a member to the pool requires reconfiguring and rebooting the client

Message Queue

Message Oriented Middleware or MOM concept involves the exchange of data between different applications using messages asynchronously. Using this mechanism, applications are decoupled and senders and receivers exist without the knowledge of each other. It becomes the responsibility of the messaging system (Message Oriented Middleware) to transfer the messages between applications. Queues allow you to store metadata for processing jobs at a later date. They can aid in the development of SOA (service-oriented architecture) by providing the flexibility to defer tasks to separate processes. When applied correctly, queues can dramatically increase the user experience of a web site by reducing load times.

Message Queue Use Case

Asynchronous: A lot of times, you don't want to or need to process a message immediately. Message queues enable asynchronous processing, which allows you to put a message on the queue without processing it immediately. Queue up as many messages as you like, then process them at your leisure.
Decoupling: It's extremely difficult to predict, at the start of a project, what the future needs of the project will be. By introducing a layer in between processes, message queues create an implicit, data-based interface that both processes implement. This allows you to extend and modify these processes independently, by simply ensuring they adhere to the same interface requirements.
Resilience: When part of your architecture fails, it doesn't need to take the entire system down with it. Message queues decouple processes, so if a process that is processing messages from the queue fails, messages can still be added to the queue to be processed when the system recovers. This ability to accept requests that will be retried or processed at a later date is often the difference between an inconvenienced customer and a frustrated customer.
Redundancy: Sometimes processes fail when processing data. Unless that data is persisted, it's lost forever. Queues mitigate this by persisting data until it has been fully processed. The put-get-delete paradigm, which many message queues use, requires a process to explicitly indicate that it has finished processing a message before the message is removed from the queue, ensuring your data is kept safe until you're done with it.

Delivery Guarantees: The redundancy provided by message queues guarantees that a message will be processed eventually, so long as a process is reading the queue. No matter how many processes are pulling data from the queue, each message will only be processed a single time. This is made possible because retrieving a message "reserves" that message, temporarily removing it from the queue. Unless the client specifically states that it's finished with that message, the message will be placed back on the queue to be processed after a configurable amount of time.

Ordering Guarantees: In a lot of situations, the order with which data is processed is important. Message queues are inherently ordered, and capable of providing guarantees that data will be processed in a specific order.

Scalability: Because message queues decouple your processes, it's easy to scale up the rate with which messages are added to the queue or processed; simply add another process. No code needs to be changed, no configurations need to be tweaked. Scaling is as simple as adding more power.

Elasticity & Spikability: When your application hits the front page of Hacker News, you're going to see unusual levels of traffic. Your application needs to be able to keep functioning with this increased load, but the traffic is anomaly, not the standard; it's wasteful to have enough resources on standby to handle these spikes. Message queues will allow beleaguered components to struggle through the increased load, instead of getting overloaded with requests and failing completely.

Buffering: In any non-trivial system, there are going to be components that require different processing times. For example, it takes less time to upload an image than it does to apply a filter to it. Message queues help these tasks operate at peak efficiency by offering a buffer layer–the process writing to the queue can write as fast as it's able to, instead of being constrained by the readiness of the process reading from the queue. This buffer helps control and optimize the speed with which data flows through your system.

Understanding Data Flow: In a distributed system, getting an overall sense of how long user actions take to complete and why is a huge problem. Message queues, through the rate with which they are processed, help to easily identify under-performing processes or areas where the data flow is not optimal.

RabbitMQ

RabbitMQ is one of the leading open-source messaging systems. It is written in Erlang, implements AMQP and is a very popular choice when messaging is involved. It supports both message persistence and replication

RabbitMQ Exchanges

Messages are not published directly to a queue, instead, the producer sends messages to an exchange. An exchange is responsible for the routing of the messages to the different queues. An exchange accepts messages from the producer application and routes them to message queues with the help of bindings and routing keys. A binding is the link between a queue and an exchange.

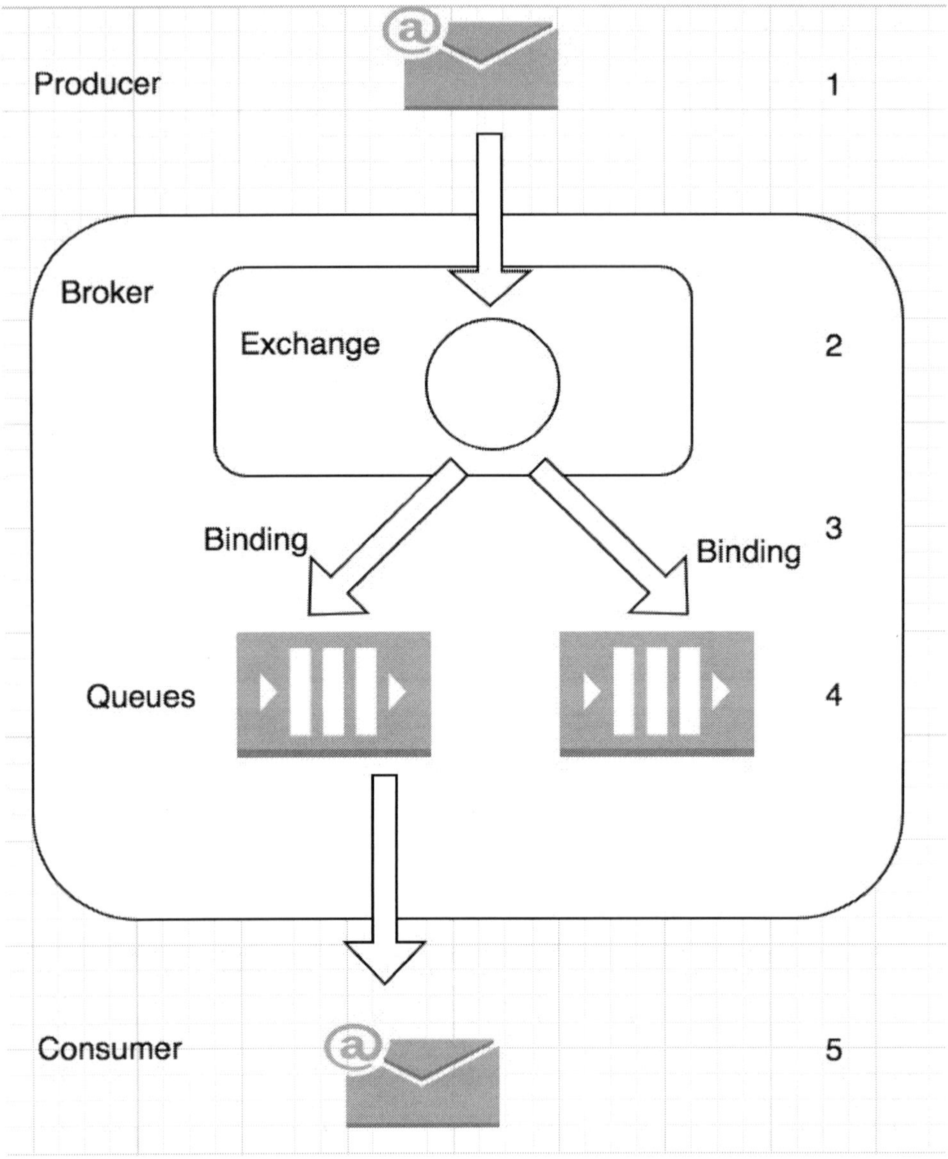

Message flow in RabbitMQ
The producer publish a message to an exchange. When you create the exchange, you have to specify the type of it. The different types of exchanges are explained in detail later on.

The exchange receives the message and is now responsible for the routing of the message. The exchange take different message attributes into account, such as routing key, depending on the exchange type.
Bindings have to be created from the exchange to queues. In this case we see two bindings to two different queues from the exchange. The Exchange routes the message in to the queues depending on message attributes.
The messages stay in the queue until they are handled by a consumer
The consumer handles the message.
Types of exchanges

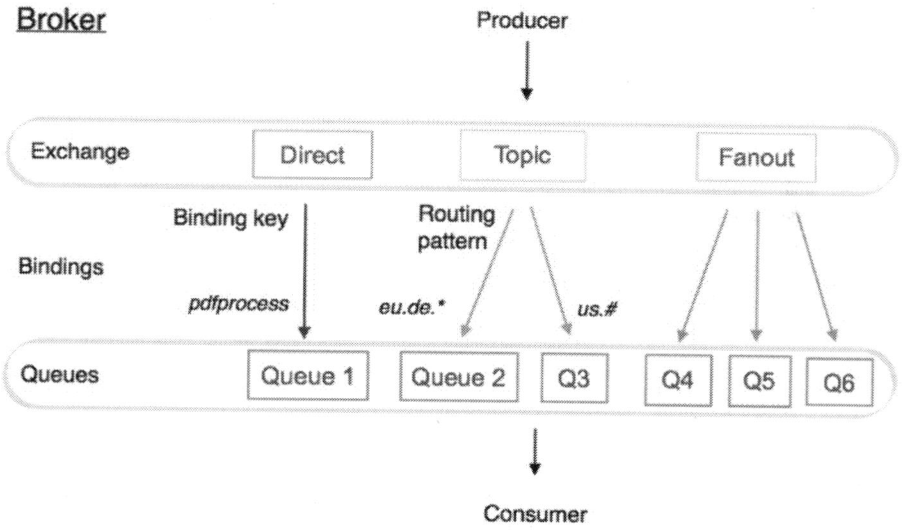

Direct: A direct exchange delivers messages to queues based on a message routing key. In a direct exchange, the message are routed to the queues whose binding key exactly matches the routing key of the message. If the queue is bound to the exchange with the binding key pdfprocess, a message published to the exchange with a routing key pdfprocess will be routed to that queue.
Fanout: A fanout exchange routes messages to all of the queues that are bound to it.
Topic: The topic exchange does a wildcard match between the routing key and the routing pattern specified in the binding.
Headers Headers exchanges use the message header attributes for routing.

Source:
https://www.cloudamqp.com/blog/2015-05-18-part1-rabbitmq-for-beginners-what-is-rabbitmq.html

Kafka

Due to the overhead associated with JMS and its various implementation and limitation with the scaling architecture, LinkedIn decided to build Kafka to address its need for monitoring activity stream data and operational metrics such as CPU, I/O usage and request timings.
In a very basic structure, a producer publishes messages to a Kafka topic (synonymous with “Messaging Queue”). A topic is also considered as a message category or feed name to which messages are published. Kafka topics are created on Kafka broker acting as Kafka server. Kafka broker also store the messages if required. Consumers then subscribe to the Kafka topic (one or more) to get the messages. Here, brokers and consumers use Zookeeper to get the state information and to track the message offsets, respectively.

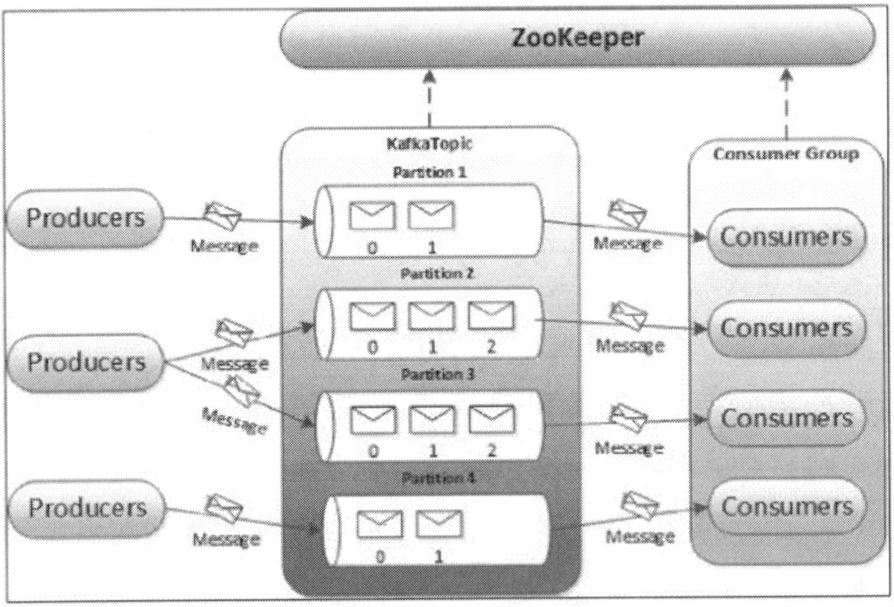

Kafka provides both pub-sub and queue based messaging system in a fast, reliable, persisted, fault-tolerance and zero downtime manner. In both cases, producers simply send the message to a topic and consumer can choose any one type of messaging system depending on their need.

Sample producer code:

```
 producer = new Producer(…);
 message = new Message("test message str".getBytes());
set = new MessageSet(message);
producer.send("topic1", set);
```

Sample consumer code:

```
streams[] = Consumer.createMessageStreams("topic1", 1)
 for (message : streams[0])
{
 bytes = message.payload();
// do something with the bytes
 }
```

Workflow of the Pub-Sub Messaging:

Producers send message to a topic at regular intervals.
Kafka broker stores all messages in the partitions configured for that particular topic. It ensures the messages are equally shared between partitions. If the producer sends two messages and there are two partitions, Kafka will store one message in the first partition and the second message in the second partition.
Consumer subscribes to a specific topic.
Once the consumer subscribes to a topic, Kafka will provide the current offset of the topic to the consumer and also saves the offset in the Zookeeper ensemble.
Consumer will request the Kafka in a regular interval (like 100 Ms) for new messages.
Once Kafka receives the messages from producers, it forwards these messages to the consumers.
Consumer will receive the message and process it.
Once the messages are processed, consumer will send an acknowledgement to the Kafka broker.
Once Kafka receives an acknowledgement, it changes the offset to the new value and updates it in the Zookeeper. Since offsets are maintained in the Zookeeper, the consumer can read next message correctly even during server outrages.
This above flow will repeat until the consumer stops the request.
Consumer has the option to rewind/skip to the desired offset of a topic at any time and read all the subsequent messages.

In a queue messaging system instead of a single consumer, a group of consumers having the same Group ID will subscribe to a topic. In simple terms, consumers subscribing to a topic with same Group ID are considered as a single group and the messages are shared among them.

Producers send message to a topic in a regular interval.
Kafka stores all messages in the partitions configured for that particular topic similar to the earlier scenario.
A single consumer subscribes to a specific topic, assume Topic-01 with Group ID as Group-1.
Kafka interacts with the consumer in the same way as Pub-Sub Messaging until new consumer subscribes the same topic, Topic-01 with the same Group ID as Group-1.
Once the new consumer arrives, Kafka switches its operation to share mode and shares the data between the two consumers. This sharing will go on until the number of con-sumers reach the number of partition configured for that particular topic.
Once the number of consumer exceeds the number of partitions, the new consumer will not receive any further message until any one of the existing consumer unsubscribes. This scenario arises because each consumer in Kafka will be assigned a minimum of one partition and once all the partitions are assigned to the existing consumers, the new consumers will have to wait.
This feature is also called as Consumer Group. In the same way, Kafka will provide the best of both the systems in a very simple and efficient manner.
Source:
Learning Apache Kafka - Second Edition-Nishant Garg

Here are some other common uses for Kafka:
Website activity tracking: The web application sends events such as page views and searches Kafka, where they become available for real-time processing, dashboards and offline analytics in Hadoop

Operational Metrics: Alerting and reporting on operational metrics. One particularly fun example is having Kafka producers and consumers occasionally publish their message counts to a special Kafka topic; a service can be used to compare counts and alert if data loss occurs.

Log aggregation: Kafka can be used across an organization to collect logs from multiple services and make them available in standard format to multiple consumers, including Hadoop and Apache Solr.

Stream processing: A framework such as Spark Streaming reads data from a topic, processes it and writes processed data to a new topic where it becomes available for users and applications. Kafka's strong durability is also very useful in the context of stream processing.

Server Side Events (SSE)

In a standard HTTP request-response scenario a client opens a connection, sends a HTTP request to the server (for example a HTTP GET request), then receives a HTTP response back and the server closes the connection once the response is fully sent/received. The initiative always comes from a client when the client requests all the data. In contrast, Server-Sent Events (SSE) is a mechanism that allows server to asynchronously push the data from the server to the client once the client-server connection is established by the client. Once the connection is established by the client, it is the server who provides the data and decides to send it to the client whenever new "chunk" of data is available. When a new data event occurs on the server, the data event is sent by the server to the client. Thus, the name Server-Sent Events. Note that at high level there are more technologies working on this principle, a short overview of the technologies supporting server-to-client communication is in this list:

Polling:
With polling a client repeatedly sends new requests to a server. If the server has no new data, then it sends appropriate indication and closes the connection. The client then waits a bit and sends another request after some time (after one second, for example).

Long-polling:
With long-polling a client sends a request to a server. If the server has no new data, it just holds the connection open and waits until data is available. Once the server has data (message) for the client, it uses the connection and sends it back to the client. Then the connection is closed.

Server-Sent events:
SSE is similar to the long-polling mechanism, except it does not send only one message per connection. The client sends a request and server holds a connection until a new message is ready, then it sends the message back to the client while still keeping the connection open so that it can be used for another message once it becomes available. Once a new message is ready, it is sent back to the client on the same initial connection. Client processes the messages sent back from the server individually without closing the connection after processing each message. So, SSE typically reuses one connection for more messages (called events). SSE also defines a dedicated media type that describes a simple format of individual events sent from

the server to the client. SSE also offers standard JavaScript client API implemented most modern browsers.

WebSocket:

WebSocket technology is different from previous technologies as it provides a real full duplex connection. The initiator is again a client which sends a request to a server with a special HTTP header that informs the server that the HTTP connection may be "upgraded" to a full duplex TCP/IP WebSocket connection. If server supports WebSocket, it may choose to do so. Once a WebSocket connection is established, it can be used for bi-directional communication between the client and the server. Both client and server can then send data to the other party at will whenever it is needed. The communication on the new WebSocket connection is no longer based on HTTP protocol and can be used for example for online gaming or any other applications that require fast exchange of small chunks of data in flowing in both directions.

Possible Applications

A few simple examples of applications that could make use of Server-Sent Events:

A real-time chart of streaming stock prices

Real-time news coverage of an important event (posting links, tweets, and images)

A live Twitter wall fed by Twitter's streaming API

A monitor for server statistics like uptime, health, and running processes

We'll use the server monitor for this article's examples. If this application were to be used in the wild, we could also check the EventSource's connection state to indicate when there's a potential problem connecting to the server.

Overview of the API

The client-side API is rather simple, and it hands-down beats the insane hacks required to get real-time events to the browser back in the bad old days.

The main points of interest:

new EventSource(url) — this creates our EventSource object, which immediately starts listening for events on the given URL.

readyState — as with XHR, we have a readyState for the EventSource that tells us if we're connecting (0), open (1), or closed (2).
onopen, onmessage — two events that we can listen for on the new EventSource object. By default, the message event will fire when new messages are received, unless the server explicitly sets the event type.
addEventListener — not only can we listen for the default message event, but we can also listen for custom messages using the addEventListener on the EventSource object, just as if we were listening for a click event.
event.data — as with most messaging APIs, the contents of the message reside in the data property of the event object. This is a string, so if we want to pass around an object, we need to encode and decode it with JSON.
close — closes the connection from the client side.
In the future, EventSource will also support CORS using an options argument to the EventSource object: { withCredentials: true }.

Simple Example

Our simple web app will notify us of server status messages — things like the load average, number of currently connected users, and most CPU-intensive processes. If I were using this application in anger, I'd probably build server modules that emit specific event types when they cross specific thresholds, so that I'm only notified when something gets to warning level.

This snippet of JavaScript connects to our server, listens for messages, and handles the data that comes with the messages:

```
var source = new EventSource('/stats');
source.onopen = function () {
  connectionOpen(true);
};

source.onerror = function () {
  connectionOpen(false);
};

source.addEventListener('connections', updateConnections, false);
source.addEventListener('requests', updateRequests, false);
source.addEventListener('uptime', updateUptime, false);

source.onmessage = function (event) {
```

  // a message without a type was fired
};

Properties of Server-Sent Events

Server-Sent Events are more than just a one-way web socket. They have some unique features:

The connection stream is from the server and read-only. This suits lots of applications, some examples of which I listed above.
They use regular HTTP requests for the persistent connection, not a special protocol, which means we can polyfill using vanilla JavaScript.
If the connection drops, the EventSource fires an error event and automatically tries to reconnect. The server can also control the timeout before the client tries to reconnect.
Clients can send a unique ID with messages. When a client tries to reconnect after a dropped connection, it will send the last known ID. Then the server can see that the client missed n messages and send the backlog of missed messages on reconnect.

Message Format

A simple message doesn't require much:

data: this is a simple message
<blank line>
Note that the end of a message is indicated by a blank line (obviously not the literal characters <blank line>).

For a message with multiple lines:

data: this is line one
data: and this is line two
You can send message IDs to be used if the connection is dropped:

id: 33
data: this is line one
data: this is line two
You can even send multiple messages in a single response so long as you separate the messages by blank lines:

id: 34

data: Remy is awesome

id: 35
data: Bruce is stinky
And you can specify your own event types (the above messages will all trigger the message event):

id: 36
event: price
data: 103.34

id: 37
event: news
data: Bruce sells his collection of replica bananas
You don't have to worry about this structure on the client side. It only applies to the server, which we will touch on next.

Typical Server

Ideally, you should use a server that has an event loop. This means you should not use Apache, but instead use a platform such as Node.js or Twisted for Python or AsyncSupport in Servlet 3.0.

Key properties:

You can only accept EventSource requests if the HTTP request says it can accept the event-stream MIME type.
You need to maintain a list of all the connected users in order to emit new events.
You should listen for dropped connections and remove them from the list of connected users.
You should optionally maintain a history of messages so that reconnecting clients can catch up on missed messages.
Here's a sample of Node.js based server. It's using Connect (a simple webby framework for Node). When it receives a request for /stats, it calls the following function. Comment is added in code so you can follow along:

```
function stats(request, response) {
  // only response to an event-stream if the request
  // actually accepts an event-stream
  if (request.headers.accept == 'text/event-stream') {
```

```
// send the header to tell the client that we're going
// to be streaming content down the connection
response.writeHead(200, {
  'content-type': 'text/event-stream',
  'cache-control': 'no-cache',
  'connection': 'keep-alive'
});

// support the polyfill - we'll come on to this later
if (request.headers['x-requested-with'] == 'XMLHttpRequest') {
  response.xhr = null;
}

// if there was a lastEventId sent in the header, send
// the history of messages we've already stored up
if (request.headers['last-event-id']) {
  var id = parseInt(request.headers['last-event-id']);
  for (var i = 0; i < history.length; i++) {
    if (history[i].id >= id) {
      sendSSE(response, history[i].id, history[i].event,
history[i].message);
    }
  }
} else {
  // if the client didn't send a lastEventId, it's the
  // first time they've come to our service, so send an
  // initial empty message with no id - this will reset
  // their id counter too.
  response.write('id\n\n');
}

// cache their connection - the response is where we write
// to send messages
connections.push(response);

// send a broadcast message to all connected clients with
// the total number of connections we have.
broadcast('connections', connections.length);

// if the connection closes to the client, remove them
// from the connections array.
```

```
request.on('close', function () {
  removeConnection(response);
});
} else {
  // if the client doesn't accept event-stream mime type,
  // send them the regular index.html page - you could do
  // anything here, including sending the client an error.
  response.writeHead(302, { location: "/index.html" });
  response.end();
}
}
```

The important trick on the server is to ensure you don't close the connection to the EventSource object. If you do, it will of course handle the closed connection, fire an error event, and try to reconnect. So you'll just want to maintain the persistent connection.

Why Not Use WebSockets?

The first is that EventSource (as we saw earlier) works over regular HTTP and can therefore be replicated entirely using JavaScript if it's not available natively. That means that we can polyfill browsers without support, like IE9.

The second is probably more important: you should always use the right technology for the job. If your real-time data is sourced from your web site, and the user doesn't interact in real-time, it's likely you need Server-Sent Events.

Source:
https://jersey.java.net/documentation/latest/sse.html
http://html5doctor.com/server-sent-events/

WebSockets

WebSockets are a bi-directional, full-duplex, persistent connection from a web browser to a server. Once a WebSocket connection is established the connection stays open until the client or server decides to close this connection. With this open connection, the client or server can send a message at any given time to the other. This makes web programming entirely event driven, not (just) user initiated. It is stateful. As well, at this time, a single running server application is aware of all connections, allowing you to communicate with any number of open connections at any given time.

WebSocket API

```
var ws = new WebSocket('wss://example.com/socket');
ws.onerror = function (error) { ... }
ws.onclose = function () { ... }

ws.onopen = function () {
        ws.send("Connection established. Hello server!");
}

ws.onmessage = function(msg) {
        if(msg.data instanceof Blob) {
                processBlob(msg.data);
        } else {
                processText(msg.data);
        }
}
```

WebRTC

WebRTC stands for web real-time communications. It is a very exciting, powerful, and highly disruptive cutting-edge technology and standard. WebRTC leverages a set of plugin-free APIs that can be used in both desktop and mobile browsers, and is progressively becoming supported by all major modern browser vendors. Previously, external plugins were required in order to achieve similar functionality as is offered by WebRTC.

WebRTC leverages multiple standards and protocols, most of which will be discussed in this article. These include data streams, STUN/TURN servers, signaling, JSEP, ICE, SIP, SDP, NAT, UDP/TCP, network sockets, and more.

Peer-To-Peer Communication

WebRTC can be used for multiple tasks, but real-time peer-to-peer audio and video (i.e., multimedia) communications is the primary benefit. In order to communicate with another person (i.e., peer) via a web browser, each person's web browser must agree to begin communication, know how to locate one another, bypass security and firewall protections, and transmit all multimedia communications in real-time.

One of the biggest challenges associated with browser-based peer-to-peer communications is knowing how to locate and establish a network socket connection with another computer's web browser in order to bidirectionally transmit multimedia data. The difficulties associated with this may not seem obvious at first, but it is explained further.

When you visit a web site, you typically enter a web address or click a link to view the page. A request is made to a server that responds by providing the web page (HTML, CSS, and JavaScript). The key here is that you make an HTTP request to a known and easily locatable (via DNS) server and get back a response (i.e., the web page).

Now let's say I wanted to have a video chat with my wife Jebar. My wife's computer is not a web server. Therefore, the problem is how do I make the request and actually receive her audio and video data directly, while also sending my audio and video data directly to her, but without going through an external server? This is where WebRTC comes into picture.

Firewalls and NAT Traversal

Most of us access the internet from a work or home-based network. Our computer typically sits behind a firewall and network access translation device (NAT), and therefore is not assigned a static public IP address. From a very high level, a NAT device translates private IP addresses from inside a firewall to public-facing IP addresses. NAT devices are needed for security and IPv4 limitations on available public IP addresses.
Here is an example of NAT at work: suppose you're at a coffee shop and join their WiFi, your computer will be assigned an IP address that exists only behind their NAT, say 172.0.23.4. To the outside world, however, your IP address may actually be 164.53.27.98. The outside world will therefore see your requests as coming from 164.53.27.98, but the NAT device will ensure responses to your requests are sent to 172.0.23.4 through the use of mapping tables. Note that in addition to the IP address, a port is also required for network communications, and the required knowledge of an accompanying port is therefore implied throughout this article.
Given the involvement of a NAT device, how do I know my mom's IP address to send audio and video data to, and likewise, how does she know what IP address to send audio and video back to?
This is where STUN (Session Traversal Utilities for NAT) and TURN (Traversal Using Relays around NAT) servers come into play. In order for WebRTC technologies to work, a request for your public-facing IP address is first made to a STUN server. Think of it like your computer asking a remote server, "Howdy, would you mind telling me what IP address you see me as having?". The server then responds with something like, "Sure thing VB, the way I see it, your IP address is 198.54.5.67".
Assuming this process works and you receive your public-facing IP address and port, you are then able to tell other peers how to contact you directly. These peers are also able to do the same thing using a STUN or TURN server and can tell you what address to contact them at as well.

Signaling, Sessions, and Protocols

The network information discovery process described above is one part of the larger topic of signaling, which is based on the JavaScript Session Establishment Protocol (JSEP) standard in the case of WebRTC. Signaling involves network discovery and NAT traversal, session creation and management, communication security, media-capability metadata and coordination, and error handling.

Signaling is not specified by the WebRTC standard, nor implemented by its APIs in order to allow flexibility in the technologies and protocols used. Signaling and the server that handles it is left to the WebRTC application creator to sort out.

Assuming that your WebRTC browser-based application is able to determine it's public-facing IP address using STUN as described, the next step is to actually negotiate and establish the network session connection with your peer. This process is analogous to making a phone call.

The initial session negotiation and establishment happens using a signaling/communication protocol specialized in multimedia communications. This protocol is also responsible for governing the rules by which the session is managed and terminated.

One such protocol is the Session Initiation Protocol (aka SIP). Note that due to the flexibility of WebRTC signaling, SIP is not the only signaling protocol that can be used. The signaling protocol chosen must also work with an application layer protocol called the Session Description Protocol (SDP), which is used in the case of WebRTC. All multimedia-specific metadata is passed using the SDP Protocol.

Any peer (i.e., WebRTC-leveraging application) that is attempting to communicate with another peer generates a set of ICE candidates, where ICE stands for the Interactive Connectivity Establishment protocol. The candidates represent a given combination of IP address, port, and transport protocol to be used. Note that a single computer may have multiple network interfaces (wireless, wired, etc.), so can be assigned multiple IP addresses, one for each interface.

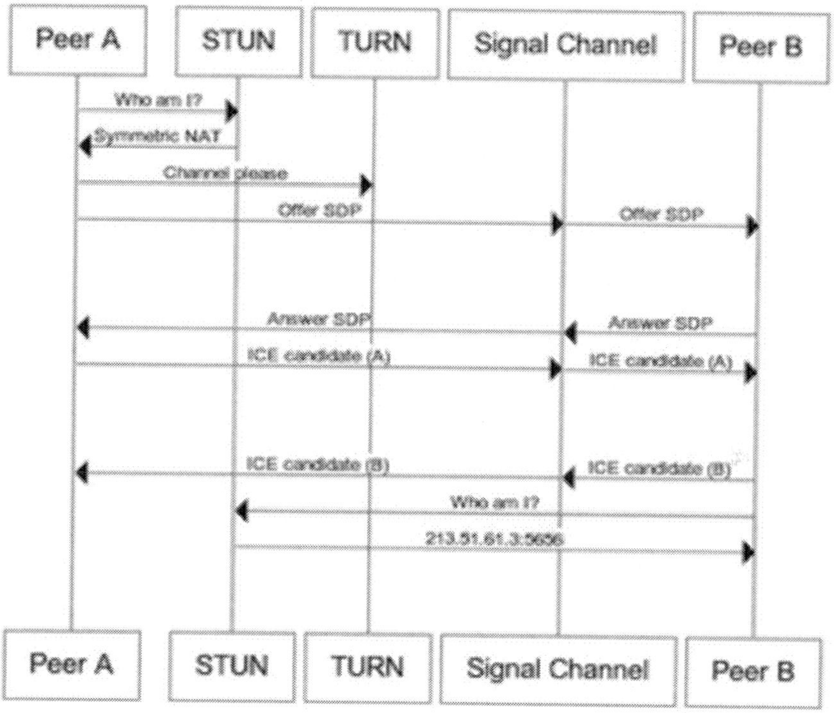

Source:
http://www.innoarchitech.com/what-is-webrtc-and-how-does-it-work/

No-SQL database

Relational databases have a long-standing position in most of the applications across different organizations which meet the required business rules and are supported by large pool of resources to implement and maintain these kinds of systems. Databases designed for today's needs are not only projected to be flexible enough to handle different data formats, but they are also expected to have extreme performance and to scale towards humongous data volumes.

RDBMS store, manage and retrieve data in relational databases through applications and queries either on the same computer or over those on the network. It holds structured data like name, address, email, telephone numbers etc. commonly known as datasets and the resulting group is defined as schema. The structured methodology of RDBMS database like SQL slows down performance as data volume or size increases and it is also not scalable to meet the needs of Big Data.
NoSQL encompasses a wide variety of different database technologies that were developed in response to a growth in the volume of data stored, the frequency, in which this data is retrieved, and performance and processing needs. It has now become an alternative to the traditional relational databases with scalability, availability with no slowdown in performance.

It's not SQL and it's not relational. Like the name suggests, it's not a replacement for a RDBMS but compliments it. NoSQL is designed for distributed data stores for very large scale data needs. Think about Facebook with its 500,000,000 users or Twitter which accumulates Terabits of data every single day.

In a NoSQL database, there is no fixed schema and no joins. A RDBMS "scales up" by getting faster and faster hardware and adding memory. NoSQL, on the other hand, can take advantage of "scaling out". Scaling out refers to spreading the load over many commodity systems. This is the component of NoSQL that makes it an inexpensive solution for large datasets.

NoSQL Categories

The current NoSQL world fits into 4 basic categories.

Key-values Stores are based primarily on Amazon's Dynamo Paper which was written in 2007. The main idea is the existence of a hash table where there is a unique key and a pointer to a particular item of data. These mappings are usually accompanied by cache mechanisms to maximize performance.

Column Family Stores were created to store and process very large amounts of data distributed over many machines. There are still keys but they point to multiple columns. In the case of BigTable (Google's Column Family NoSQL model), rows are identified by a row key with the data sorted and stored by this key. The columns are arranged by column family.

Document Databases were inspired by Lotus Notes and are similar to key-value stores. The model is basically versioned documents that are collections of other key-value collections. The semi-structured documents are stored in formats like JSON.

Graph Databases are built with nodes, relationships between notes and the properties of nodes. Instead of tables of rows and columns and the rigid structure of SQL, a flexible graph model is used which can scale across many machines.

Major NoSQL Players

The major players in NoSQL have emerged primarily because of the organizations that have adopted them. Some of the largest NoSQL technologies include:

Dynamo: Dynamo was created by Amazon.com and is the most prominent Key-Value NoSQL database. Amazon was in need of a highly scalable distributed platform for their e-commerce businesses so they developed Dynamo. Amazon S3 uses Dynamo as the storage mechanism.

Cassandra: Cassandra was open sourced by Facebook and is a column oriented NoSQL database.

MongoDB: Cross-platform document-oriented database system that eschews the traditional table-based relational database structure in favor of JSON-like documents with dynamic schemas making the integration of data in certain types of applications easier and faster.

BigTable: BigTable is Google's proprietary column oriented database. Google allows the use of BigTable but only for the Google App Engine.

SimpleDB: SimpleDB is another Amazon database. Used for Amazon EC2 and S3, it is part of Amazon Web Services that charges fees depending on usage.

CouchDB: CouchDB along with MongoDB are open source document oriented NoSQL databases.

Neo4J: Neo4j is an open source graph database.

Benefits of NoSQL Database

Using NoSQL database for processing big data has several advantages. Some of the key benefits are:

Elastic Scaling: Earlier with relational database, database administrators always depend on scaling-up or purchasing larger, expensive, multiple servers, as the database load increased, rather than scaling-out or distributing the data across multiple hosts. The new classes of NoSQL databases are aimed to expand transparently and horizontally, to consider the advantage of new nodes and it is generally designed, keeping in mind, the low-cost commodity hardware.

Bigger Data Handling Capability: RDBMS capacity has been increasing to match the growth in volumes of data, but the boundaries of data volumes that can be handled by a single RDBMS are insufficient for some enterprises. NoSQL distributed databases allow data to be spread through thousands of servers with little reduction in performance. And it exceeds that of other databases, which can be controlled by the biggest RDBMS. Features like automatic repair, relaxed data distribution, and simpler data models make administration and tuning requirements lesser in NoSQL.

Cost Effective: NoSQL databases usually use clusters of inexpensive commodity servers, to manage the humongous data and transaction volumes, while RDBMS inclines to rely on expensive servers and storage systems. Therefore, the processing and storing data cost per terabyte in case of NoSQL can be many times lesser than the cost of RDBMS.

No Schema or Fixed Data Model: Data can be inserted in a NoSQL database without defining an inflexible database schema. The data being inserted or the data model can be restructured any time, without application disruption. This offers immense application and business flexibility. But on the other side, change management is a challenge in SQL. In NoSQL, even trivial changes to the data model have to be wisely managed and may require downtime or reduced service levels.

Integrated Caching Facility: To increase data output and performance improvement, NoSQL techniques cache data in system memory. This is different to SQL database, where this kind on caching has to be performed using separate infrastructure.

Cassandra vs. DynamoDB

Capacity and Replication Planning

In order to plan capacity with Cassandra one must understand the performance of a single node, performance impact of replication across more than one, and consistency when more than one node is involved. There is no document that says "If you provision this instance type on AWS and configure it in this way you will get these many operations per second."

There is a multitude of settings in the configuration files that require a graduate degree in computer science to comprehend and that are best left alone at their defaults. In other words, there is no sure way for me to say that if I want this many concurrent users doing this many concurrent operations I need this type of a cluster.

Contrasting that with DynamoDB, as far as capacity planning goes all I need to care about is what is the minimum IOPS require by my application of the particular table, what is the maximum I am willing to pay for, and how often and when I should auto scale it. Period. End of story.

Consistency

In Cassandra world consistency revolves around two factors: consistency level and replication factor. You can have fast performance and eventual consistency, or you can have slower performance and high consistency. While consistency level is specified per call, replication factor is specified at key space initialization. If you ever want to change replication factor be prepared for hours of maintenance work which becomes impossible on a live cluster once the number of nodes grows.

Again, this is an area where DynamoDB model makes much more sense. If I want consistent reads I must pay twice for IOPS. That's it. It becomes a purely financial decision.

Scaling up and down

Scaling a Cassandra cluster involves adding new nodes. Each additional node requires hours of baby-sitting. The process of adding a node takes a few mins, but bootstrapping can take hours. If you are using tokens you are in a bigger pickle since you have to compute just the right balance, move tokens around, and clean up (* we are using tokens since this is a legacy production cluster, and there is no safe and easy way to migrate to vnodes). Once you have added a node, it becomes a fixed cost plus extra network charges. If you ever want to scale down you have to work backwards and decommission extra nodes, which takes hours, and then you have to rebalance your cluster again if you're still using tokens.

The tokens vs vnodes situation is of particular annoyance to me. Cassandra has left many of us excluded from this feature because it does not offer clean, safe and seamless upgrade mechanism.

Going back to DynamoDB, the only thing I need to care about is IOPS. What is my minimum? What is my maximum? How much am I willing to pay. Period. End of story.

Software upgrades

Each time I had to upgrade Cassandra the process was the same and tedious: go to each node, upgrade the software, verify the settings have migrated (Cassandra does not offer tools to cleanly port settings from older versions), start the new binaries, run upgrade ss-tables process. It is a process that is bound to ruin a weekend for me. I am simply no longer interested.

One of the pet annoyances I have with Cassandra is how they deprecated Thrift API. Many of us have used the software for years and now have to either use deprecated API or port code to new CQL. Some of us have chosen, wisely or not, to use a Thrift library that is no longer up to date. So, to use the new API we have to port the code, and an obvious question comes up – if I have to port my code to new library, do I still want to use Cassandra?

I do not need to concern myself with software upgrades with DynamoDB. Period. End of story.

Node replacements

This is similar to scaling, as I described above. Node replacement in Cassandra world is an hours long process. No such thing with DynamoDB.

Regular repairs

If a cluster grows larger, especially in multi data center scenarios, Cassandra recommends that a regular repair process is run on each node. Again, this is a long running process that imposes significant IO workload on all nodes in the cluster. It can run for days on end, results in extra disk utilization, and requires baby-sitting. On more than one occasion it has ruined a weekend for me.

DynamoDB does not require me to do anything of the sort.

Conclusion:

From the data model perspective, DynamoDB and Cassandra are very similar. Cassandra offers more flexibility for sure, and I would much prefer Cassandra over DynamoDB. However, with no managed offering that is as simple as DynamoDB I really don't have the patience anymore.

Cassandra vs. MongoDB

Are you considering Cassandra or MongoDB as the data store for your next project? Would you like to compare the two databases? Cassandra and MongoDB are both "NoSQL" databases, but the reality is that they are very different. They have very different strengths and value propositions – so any comparison has to be a nuanced one. Let's start with initial requirements… Neither of these databases replace RDBMS, nor are they "ACID" databases. So, If you have a transactional workload where normalization and consistency are the primary requirements, neither of these databases will work for you. You are better off sticking with traditional relational databases like MySQL, PostGres, Oracle etc. Now that we have relational databases out of the way, let's consider the major differences between Cassandra and MongoDB that will help you make the decision. In this post, I am not going to discuss specific features but will point out some high-level strategic differences to help you make your choice.

1. Expressive Object Model

MongoDB supports a rich and expressive object model. Objects can have properties and objects can be nested in one another (for multiple levels). This model is very "object oriented" and can easily represent any object structure in your domain. You can also index the property of any object at any level of the hierarchy – this is strikingly powerful! Cassandra, on the other hand, offers a fairly traditional table structure with rows and columns. Data is more structured and each column has a specific type which can be specified during creation.

Verdict: If your problem domain needs a rich data model then MongoDB is a better fit for you.

2. Secondary Indexes

Secondary indexes are a first class construct in MongoDB. This makes it easy to index any property of an object stored in MongoDB even if it is nested. This makes it really easy to query based on these secondary indexes. Cassandra has only cursory support for secondary indexes. Secondary indexes are also limited to single columns and equality comparisons. If you are mostly going to be querying by the primary key then Cassandra will work well for you.

Verdict: If your application needs secondary indexes and needs flexibility in the query model then MongoDB is a better fit for you.

3. High Availability

MongoDB supports a "single master" model. This means you have a master node and a number of slave nodes. In case the master goes down, one of the slaves is elected as master. This process happens automatically but it takes time, usually 10-40 seconds. During this time of new leader election, your replica set is down and cannot take writes. This works for most applications but ultimately depends on your needs. Cassandra supports a "multiple master" model. The loss of a single node does not affect the ability of the cluster to take writes – so you can achieve 100% uptime for writes.

Verdict: If you need 100% uptime Cassandra is a better fit for you.

4. Write Scalability

MongoDB with its "single master" model can take writes only on the primary. The secondary servers can only be used for reads. So essentially if you have three node replicas set, only the master is taking writes and the other two nodes are only used for reads. This greatly limits write scalability. You can deploy multiple shards but essentially only 1/3 of your data nodes can take writes. Cassandra with its "multiple master" model can take writes on any server. Essentially your write scalability is limited by the number of servers you have in the cluster. The more servers you have in the cluster, the better it will scale.

Verdict: If write scalability is your thing, Cassandra is a better fit for you.

5. Query Language Support

Cassandra supports the CQL query language which is very similar to SQL. If you already have a team of data analysts, they will be able to port over a majority of their SQL skills which is very important to large organizations. However, CQL is not full blown ANSI SQL – It has several limitations (No join support, no OR clauses) etc. MongoDB at this point has no support for a query language. The queries are structured as JSON fragments.

Verdict: If you need query language support, Cassandra is the better fit for you.

6. Performance Benchmarks

Let's talk performance. At this point, you are probably expecting a performance benchmark comparison of the databases. I have deliberately not included performance benchmarks in the comparison. In any comparison, we have to make sure we are making an apples-to-apples comparison.

1. Database model - The database model/schema of the application being tested makes a big difference. Some schemas are well suited for MongoDB and some are well suited for Cassandra. So when comparing databases, it is important to use a model that works reasonably well for both databases.

2. Load characteristics – The characteristics of the benchmark load are very important. E.g. In write-heavy benchmarks, I would expect Cassandra to smoke MongoDB. However, in read-heavy benchmarks, MongoDB and Cassandra should be similar in performance.

3. Consistency requirements - This is a tricky one. You need to make sure that the read/write consistency requirements specified are identical in both databases and not biased towards one participant. Very often in a number of the 'Marketing' benchmarks the knobs are tune to disadvantage the other side. So pay close attention to the consistency settings.

One last thing to keep in mind is that the benchmark load may or may not reflect the performance of your application. So, in order for benchmarks to be useful, it is very important to find a benchmark load that reflects the performance characteristics of your application. Here are some benchmarks you might want to look at: https://www.mongodb.com/scale/nosql-performance-benchmarks http://www.datastax.com/nosql-databases/benchmarks-cassandra-vs-mongodb-vs-Hbase

7. Ease of Use

If you had asked this question a couple of years ago MongoDB would be the hands down winner. It's a fairly simple task to get MongoDB up and running. In the last couple of years, however, Cassandra has made great strides in this aspect of the product. With the adoption of CQL as the primary interface for Cassandra it has taken this a step further – they have made it very simple for legions of SQL programmers to use Cassandra very easily.

Verdict: Both are fairly easy to use and ramp up.

8. Native Aggregation

MongoDB has a built-in Aggregation framework to run an ETL pipeline to transform the data stored in the database. This is great for small to medium jobs but as your data processing needs become more complicated the aggregation framework becomes difficult to debug. Cassandra does not have a built-in aggregation framework. External tools like Hadoop, Spark are used for this.

9. Schema-less Models

In MongoDB, you can choose to not enforce any schema on your documents. While this was the default in prior versions in the newer version you have the option to enforce a schema for your documents. Each document in MongoDB can be a different structure and it is up to your application to interpret the data. While this is not relevant to most applications, in some cases the extra flexibility is important. Cassandra in the newer versions (with CQL as the default language) provides static typing. You need to define the type of very column upfront.

MicroServices

The idea behind microservices is that some types of applications become easier to build and maintain when they are broken down into smaller, composable pieces which work together. Each component is developed separately, and the application is then simply the sum of its constituent components. This is in contrast to a traditional, "monolithic" application which is all developed all in one piece.

There are many reasons why this approach is considered an easier way to develop large applications, particular enterprise applications, and various types of software as a service delivered over the Internet.

One of the reasons is from a project engineering perspective. When the different components of an application are separated, they can be developed concurrently. Another is resilience. Rather than relying upon a single virtual or physical machine, components can be spread around multiple severs or even multiple data centers. If a component dies, you spin up another, and the rest of the application can continue to function. It allows more efficient scaling, as rather than scaling up with bigger and more powerful machines, or just more copies of the entire application, you can scale out with duplicate copies of the heaviest-used parts.

The common definition of microservices generally relies upon each microservice providing an API endpoint, often but not always a stateless REST API which can be accessed over HTTP(S) just like a standard webpage. This method for accessing microservices make them easy for developers to consume as they only require tools and methods many developers are already familiar with.

Microservices depend not just on the technology being set up to support this concept, but on an organization having the culture, know-how, and structures in place for development teams to be able to adopt this model. Microservices are a part of a larger shift in IT departments towards a DevOps culture, in which development and operations teams work closely together to support an application over its lifecycle, and go through a rapid or even continuous release cycle rather than a more traditional long cycle.

Many people see Docker or other container technologies as enablers of a microservice architecture.

Unlike virtual machines, containers are designed to be pared down to the minimal viable pieces needed to run whatever the one thing the container is designed to do, rather than packing multiple functions into the same virtual or physical machine. The ease of development that Docker and similar tools provide help make possible rapid development and testing of services.

Of course, containers are just a tool, and microservice architecture is just a concept. So, it is entirely possible to build an application which could be described as following a microservices approach without using containers, just as it would be possible to build a much more traditional application inside of a container (although this may not be a good idea).
In order to actually run an application based on microservices, you need to be able monitor, manage, and scale the different constituent parts. There are a number of different tools that might allow you to accomplish this. For containers, open source tools like Kubernetes, Docker Swarm, or Apache projects like Mesos or ZooKeeper might be a part of your solution.

Docker

Docker is an open platform for developers and sysadmins to build, ship, and run distributed applications. In other, simpler words, Docker is a container manager. Note that it's not a virtualization solution that abstracts away the underlying OS or hardware, like the well-known VirtualBox, but an engine to package an individual application system to run in its own particular environment.

Docker is excellent for microservices, as it isolates containers to one process or service. This intentional containerization of single services or processes makes it very simple to manage and update these services. Therefore, it's not surprising that the next wave on top of Docker has led to the emergence of frameworks for the sole purpose of managing more complex scenarios, such as: how to manage single services in a cluster, or multiple instances in a service across hosts, or how to coordinate between multiple services on a deployment and management level.

Containers make it very easy to run cloud-native applications on physical or virtual infrastructure. They are lighter weight compared to VMs and make more efficient use of the underlying infrastructure. Containers are meant to make it easy to turn apps on and off to meet fluctuating demand and move apps seamlessly between different environments or even clouds. While the container runtime APIs meet the needs of managing one container on one host, they are not suited to manage multiple containers deployed on multiple hosts. This is where we need to look at container orchestration tools.

Container Orchestration tools can manage complex, multi-container apps deployed on a cluster of machines. These tools can treat an entire cluster as a single entity for deployment and management. Container orchestration tools can automate all aspects from initial placement, scheduling and deployment to updates and health monitoring functions that support scaling and failover.

Capabilities of Container Orchestration Tools

Here are some of the main capabilities that a modern container orchestration platform will typically provide

Provisioning

Container orchestration tools can provision or schedule containers within the cluster and launch them. As part of this, the tool will determine the right placement for the containers by selecting an appropriate host based on the specified constraints such as resource requirements, location affinity etc. The underlying goal is to increase utilization of the available resources. Most tools will be agnostic to the underlying infrastructure provider and, in theory, should be able to move containers across environments and clouds.

Configuration-as-text

Container orchestration tools can load the application blueprint from a schema defined in YAML or JSON. These are popular languages to define infrastructure-as-code similar to OpenStack Heat templates, Puppet Manifests or Chef recipes. Defining the blueprint in this manner makes it easy for DevOps teams to edit, share and version the configurations and provide repeatable deployments across development, testing and production.

Monitoring

Container orchestration tools will track and monitor the health of the containers and hosts in the cluster. If a container crashes, a new one can be spun up quickly. If a host fails, the tool will restart the failed containers on another host. It will also run specified health checks at the appropriate frequency and update the list of available nodes based on the results. In short, the tool will ensure that the current state of the cluster matches the configuration specified.

Rolling Upgrades and Rollback

One of the most desired ability is for the orchestration tool to perform 'rolling upgrades' of the application where a new version is applied incrementally across the cluster. Traffic is routed appropriately as containers go down temporarily to receive the update. A rolling update guarantees a minimum number of "ready" containers at any point, so that all old containers are not replaced if there aren't enough healthy new containers to replace them. If, however, the new version doesn't perform as expected then the orchestration tool can also rollback the applied change.

Policies for Placement, Scalability etc.

Container orchestration tools provide a way to define policies for host placement, security, performance and high availability. When configured correctly, container orchestration platforms can enable organizations to deploy and operate containerized application workloads in a secure, reliable and scalable way. For example, an application can be scaled up automatically based on CPU usage of the containers.

Service Discovery

Since containers encourage a microservices based architecture, service discovery becomes a critical function and is provided in different ways by container orchestration platforms e.g. DNS or proxy-based etc. For example, a web application front-end dynamically discovering another microservice or a database.

Ease of Administration

Container orchestration tools themselves should be easy to deploy, configure and setup for Administrators. They should connect to existing IT tools for SSO, RBAC etc. An extensible architecture will connect to external systems such as local or cloud storage, networking systems etc.

This was a brief overview of the importance of choosing the right container orchestration tool to deploy and manage cloud-native applications. Let's discuss and compare some of the popular tools such as Kubernetes vs Mesos and Kubernetes vs Docker swarm.

Docker Swarm

Docker Swarm provides native clustering capabilities to turn a group of Docker engines into a single, virtual Docker Engine. Swarm uses the standard Docker API, so normal docker run commands can be used to launch containers and Swarm will take care of selecting an appropriate host to run the container on. Other tools that use the Docker API, e.g. Docker Compose, can use Swarm without any changes.

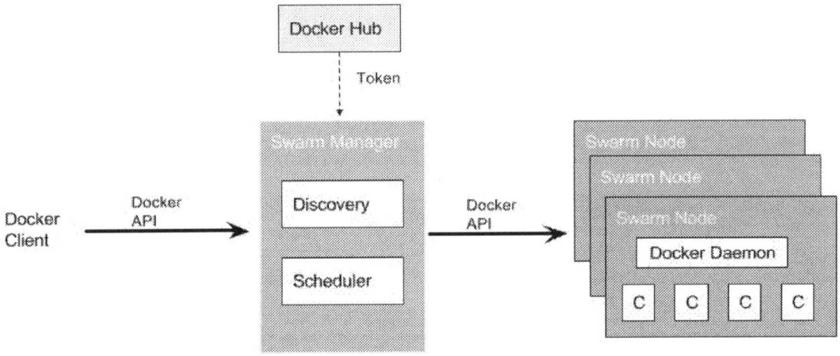

Each host in a Swarm cluster runs a Swarm agent and one host runs a Swarm manager. The manager will orchestrate and schedule containers on the hosts. Similar to other container orchestration tools, a Discovery service will find and add new hosts to the cluster. Third-party tools like Consul, ZooKeeper, etc are required to ensure high availability and failover to a secondary Swarm manager.

Kubernetes

With Kubernetes you can easily deploy and manage multiple Docker containers of the same type through an intelligent tagging system. You basically describe the characteristics of the image you'd like to deploy—e.g. number of instances, CPU, RAM—and Kubernetes will allocate it for you based on what is physically available on the set of hosts you're deploying too. You don't need to care where these are located physically, since the tagging system enables you to uniquely identify your images. On top of the tagging, you can create another level of grouping called "pods" that are essentially a continuous query for containers that have one or more tags. Kubernetes constantly updates the set of containers that satisfy the query and implements load balancing across these containers so that there's a single endpoint for anyone accessing them from the outside.

Kubernetes architecture diagram and the following explanation.

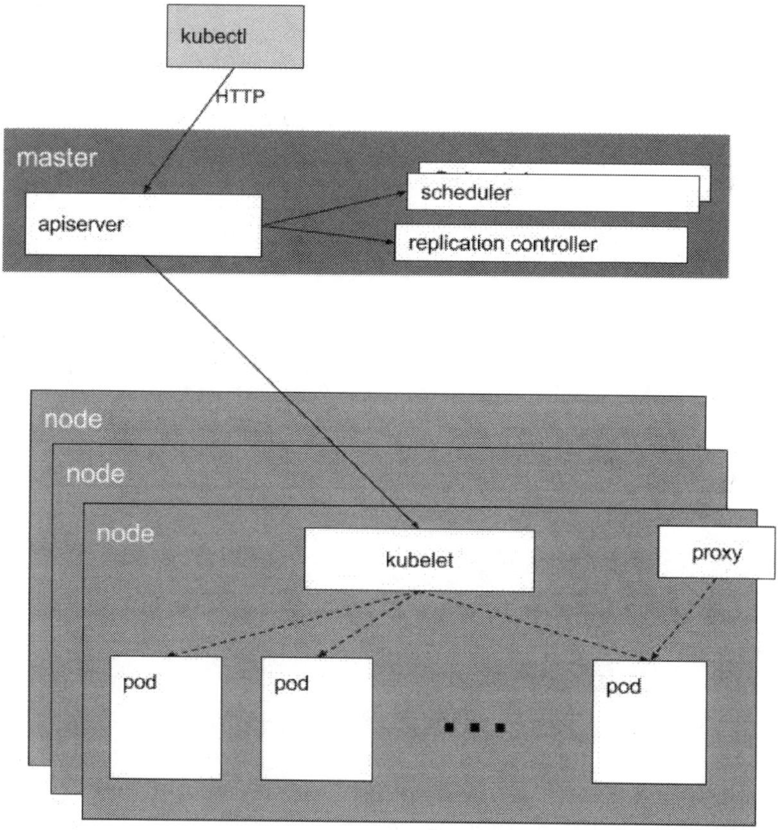

The major components in a Kubernetes cluster are:

Pods – Kubernetes deploys and schedules containers in groups called pods. A pod will typically include 1 to 5 containers that collaborate to provide a service.

Flat Networking Space – The default network model in Kubernetes is flat and permits all pods to talk to each other. Containers in the same pod share an IP and can communicate using ports on the localhost address.
Labels – Labels are key-value pairs attached to objects and can be used to search and update multiple objects as a single set.
Services – Services are endpoints that can be addressed by name and can be connected to pods using label selectors. The service will automatically round-robin requests between the pods. Kubernetes will set up a DNS server for the cluster that watches for new services and allows them to be addressed by name.
Replication Controllers – Replication controllers are the way to instantiate pods in Kubernetes. They control and monitor the number of running pods for a service, improving fault tolerance.

This is all very useful when it comes to simple, stateless services that you can load balance across, and where all instances are completely identical. A good example for such a service would be web service of some sort or a stateless web application.

Things get a bit more complicated when you have stateful services, or when the microservice itself is composed of multiple pieces—such as a database or a messaging queue. Kubernetes has an implicit assumption that all the state that is shared between service instances (e.g. a Mongo cluster that stores user profiles) is managed outside of Kubernetes.

However, in many cases, what you want to manage is composed of multiple tiers (web, database, messaging, etc) that are dependent on one another. And as such, often times, this will be tough if not impossible to do with Kubernetes. Kubernetes is designed for a situation where each container is literally self-contained, and replicable; many times this isn't necessarily the case. This is also true if you want to automate the deployment and management of application tiers that are not microservices—like a central data repository, e.g. a Hadoop or Cassandra. The latter two cannot be deployed on top of Kubernetes (although something simpler such a Redis can be).

In such a case you'd need an orchestrator capable of describing more complex topologies and deployments—and this is where TOSCA (Topology Orchestration Specification for Cloud Applications) comes into the mix.

The idea with TOSCA is to deploy each piece in the most ideal approach for it. If it's a simple stateless microservice, then the best method is to use Docker and Kubernetes (or the likes of it). When you're dealing with more complex topologies that require intricate orchestration (e.g. a fully replicated and sharded mongo cluster, or a more complex microservice), this would be the scenario to use a TOSCA blueprint. Naturally, a TOSCA blueprint can also be used for the former case (i.e. spawn a few instances of a Docker image) if you want to stick with a single way of doing things.

An example of this kind of implementation is with the Cloudify Docker orchestration plugin that leverages TOSCA for simple microservices deployment (using TOSCA output parameters as means to expose a specific service's endpoint) and more complex topologies through support for the orchestration of complex application stacks. Based on this approach, you also get the side benefit of support for post-deployment concerns, e.g. auto scaling, monitoring and auto-healing, that are made possible through Cloudify's TOSCA-based blueprints.

Compare Kubernetes vs Docker Swarm

	Kubernetes	Docker Swarm
Types of Workloads	Cloud Native applications	Cloud Native applications
Applicatio n Definition	A combination of Pods, Replication Controllers, Replica Sets, Services and Deployments. As explained in the overview above, a pod is a group of co-located containers; the atomic unit of deployment.	Apps defined in Docker Compose can be deployed on a Swarm cluster
	Pods do not express dependencies among individual containers within them.	The built-in scheduler has several filters such as node tags, affinity and strategies that will assign containers to the underlying nodes so as to maximize

		performance and resource utilization.
	Containers in a single Pod are guaranteed to run on a single Kubernetes node.	
Application Scalability constructs	Each application tier is defined as a pod and can be scaled when managed by a Deployment or Replication Controller. The scaling can be manual or automated.	Possible to scale individual containers defined in the Compose file.
High Availability	Pods are distributed among Worker Nodes.	Containers are distributed among Swarm Nodes.
	Services also HA by detecting unhealthy pods and removing them.	The Swarm manager is responsible for the entire cluster and manages the resources of multiple Docker hosts at scale.
		To ensure the Swarm manager is highly available, a single primary manager instance and multiple replica instances must be created. Requests issued on a replica are automatically proxied to the primary manager.
		If a primary manager fails, tools like Consul, ZooKeeper or etcd will pick a replica as the new manager.

Load Balancing	Pods are exposed through a Service, which can be a load balancer.	Load balancer is typically just another service defined in a Compose file. The swarm manager uses ingress load balancing to expose the services you want to make available externally to the swarm. Internally, the swarm lets you specify how to distribute service containers between nodes.
Auto-scaling for the Application	Auto-scaling using a simple number-of-pods target is defined declaratively with the API exposed by Replication Controllers. CPU-utilization-per-pod target is available as of v1.1 in the Scale subresource. Other targets are on the roadmap.	Not directly available. For each service, you can declare the number of tasks you want to run. When you scale up or down, the swarm manager automatically adapts by adding or removing tasks to maintain the desired state.

Rolling Application Upgrades and Rollback	"Deployment" model supports strategies, but one similar to Mesos is planned for the future	At rollout time, you can apply service updates to nodes incrementally. The swarm manager lets you control the delay between service deployment to different sets of nodes. If anything goes wrong, you can roll-back a task to a previous version of the service.
	Health checks test for liveness i.e. is app responsive	
Logging and monitoring	Health checks of two kinds: liveness (is app responsive) and readiness (is app responsive, but busy preparing and not yet able to serve)	Logging: Can ship logs to ELK deployed in cluster

	Logging: Container logs shipped to Elasticsearch/Kibana (ELK) service deployed in cluster	Monitoring: Can use external tools, e.g. Riemann
	Resource usage monitoring: Heapster/Grafana/Influx service deployed in cluster	
	Logging/monitoring add-ons are part of official project	
	Sysdig Cloud integration	
Storage	Two storage APIs:	Docker Engine and Swarm support mounting volumes into a container.
	The first provides abstractions for individual storage backends (e.g. NFS, AWS EBS, ceph,flocker).	
		A volume is stored locally by default. Volume plugins (e.g.flocker) mount volumes on networked storage (e.g., AWS EBS, cinder, ceph)
	The second provides an abstraction for a storage resource request (e.g. 8 Gb), which can be fulfilled with different storage backends.	

	Modifying the storage resource used by the Docker daemon on a cluster node requires temporarily removing the node from the cluster	
Networking	The networking model lets any pod can communicate with other pods and with any service.	Docker Engine can create overlay networks on a single host. Docker Swarm can create overlay networks that span hosts in the cluster. By default, nodes in the swarm encrypt traffic between themselves and other nodes.
	The model requires two networks (one for pods, the other for services)	A container can be assigned an IP on an overlay network. Containers that use the same overlay network can communicate, even if they are running on different hosts.
	Neither network is assumed to be (or needs to be) reachable from outside the cluster.	
	The most common way of meeting this requirement is to deploy an overlay network on the cluster nodes.	

Service Discovery	Pods discover services using intra-cluster DNS	Swarm manager node assigns each service a unique DNS name and load balances running containers. You can query every container running in the swarm through a DNS server embedded in the swarm.
		Docker Swarm comes with multiple discovery backends
		Docker Hub as a hosted discovery service is intended to be used for dev/test. Not recommended for production
		A static file or list of nodes can be used as a discovery backend. The file must be stored on a host that is accessible from the Swarm manager. You can also pass a node list as an option when you start Swarm.
		The recommended way to do node discovery in Swarm is Docker's libkv project. The project supports: Consul 0.5.1 or higher, Etcd 2.0 or higher, ZooKeeper 3.4.5 or higher.
Performance and scalability	With the release of 1.2, Kubernetes now supports 1000-node clusters. Kubernetes scalability is benchmarked against the following Service Level Objectives (SLOs):	According to the Swarm website, Swarm is production ready and tested to scale up to one thousand (1,000) nodes and fifty thousand (50,000) containers with no performance degradation in spinning up incremental containers onto the node cluster.

	API responsiveness: 99% of all API calls return in less than 1s	Check out these other blogs on the topic-
	Pod startup time: 99% of pods and their containers (with pre-pulled images) start within 5s.	https://blog.docker.com/2015/11/scale-testing-docker-swarm-30000-containers/
		https://medium.com/on-docker/evaluating-container-platforms-at-scale-5e7b44d93f2c#.sblte6chl

Mesos (+Marathon)

Apache Mesos is an open-source cluster manager designed to scale to very large clusters, from hundreds to thousands of hosts. Mesos supports diverse kinds of workloads such as Hadoop tasks, cloud native applications etc. The architecture of Mesos is designed around high-availability and resilience.

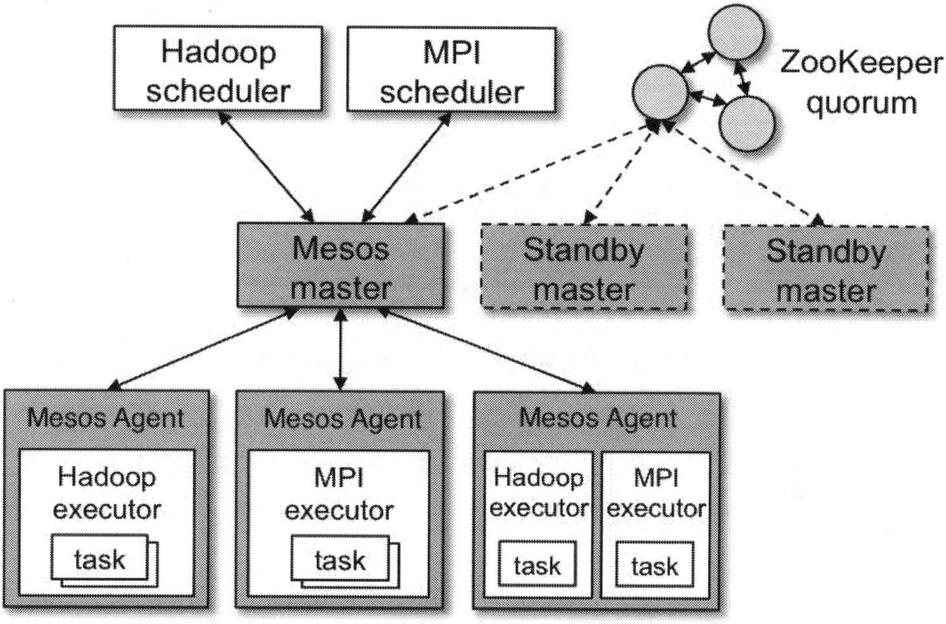

The major components in a Mesos cluster are:

Mesos Agent Nodes – Responsible for actually running tasks. All agents submit a list of their available resources to the master.
Mesos Master – The master is responsible for sending tasks to the agents. It maintains a list of available resources and makes "offers" of them to frameworks e.g. Hadoop. The master decides how many resources to offer based on an allocation strategy. There will typically be stand-by master instances to take over in case of a failure.
ZooKeeper – Used in elections and for looking up address of current master. Multiple instances of ZooKeeper are run to ensure availability and handle failures.
Frameworks – Frameworks co-ordinate with the master to schedule tasks onto agent nodes. Frameworks are composed of two parts-
the executor process runs on the agents and takes care of running the tasks and
the scheduler registers with the master and selects which resources to use based on offers from the master.

There may be multiple frameworks running on a Mesos cluster for different kinds of task. Users wishing to submit jobs interact with frameworks rather than directly with Mesos.

In the figure above, a Mesos cluster is running alongside the Marathon, framework as the scheduler. The Marathon scheduler uses ZooKeeper to locate the current Mesos master which it will submit tasks to. Both the Marathon scheduler and the Mesos master have stand-bys ready to start work should the current master become unavailable.

Marathon, created by Mesosphere, is designed to start, monitor and scale long-running applications, including cloud native apps. Clients interact with Marathon through a REST API. Other features include support for health checks and an event stream that can be used to integrate with load-balancers or for analyzing metrics.

Comparison Between Kubernetes and Mesos(+Marathon)

	Kubernetes	Mesos
Types of Workloads	Cloud Native applications	Support for diverse kinds of workloads such as big data, cloud native apps etc.
Application Definition	A combination of Pods, Replication Controllers, Replica Sets, Services and Deployments. As explained in the overview above, a pod is a group of co-located containers; the atomic unit of deployment.	"Application Group" models dependencies as a tree of groups. Components are started in dependency order.
	Pods do not express dependencies among individual containers within them.	Colocation of group's containers on same Mesos slave is not supported.
	Containers in a single Pod are guaranteed to run on a single Kubernetes node.	A Pod abstraction is on roadmap, but not yet available.

Application Scalability constructs	Each application tier is defined as a pod and can be scaled when managed by a Deployment or Replication Controller. The scaling can be manual or automated.	Possible to scale an individual group, its dependents in the tree are also scaled.
High Availability	Pods are distributed among Worker Nodes.	Applications are distributed among Slave Nodes.
	Services also HA by detecting unhealthy pods and removing them.	
Load Balancing	Pods are exposed through a Service, which can be a load balancer.	Application can be reached via Mesos-DNS, which can act as a rudimentary load balancer.
Auto-scaling for the Application	Auto-scaling using a simple number-of-pods target is defined declaratively with the API exposed by Replication Controllers.	Load-sensitive autoscaling available as a proof-of-concept application.
	CPU-utilization-per-pod target is available as of v1.1 in the Scale subresource. Other targets are on the roadmap.	Rate-sensitive autoscaling available for Mesosphere's enterprise customers.
		Rich metric-based scaling policy.
Rolling Application Upgrades and Rollback	"Deployment" model supports strategies, but one similar to Mesos is planned for the future	"Rolling restarts" model uses application-defined minimumHealthCapacity (ratio of nodes serving new/old application)
	Health checks test for liveness i.e. is app	"Health check" hooks consume a "health" API

	responsive	provided by the application itself
Logging and monitoring	Health checks of two kinds: liveness (is app responsive) and readiness (is app responsive, but busy preparing and not yet able to serve)	Logging: Can use ELK
	Logging: Container logs shipped to Elasticsearch/Kibana (ELK) service deployed in cluster	Monitoring: Can use external tools
	Resource usage monitoring: Heapster/Grafana/Influx service deployed in cluster	
	Logging/monitoring add-ons are part of official project	
	Sysdig Cloud integration	
Storage	Two storage APIs:	A Marathon container can use persistent volumes, but such volumes are local to the node where they are created, so the container must always run on that node.
	The first provides abstractions for individual storage backends (e.g. NFS, AWS EBS, ceph,flocker).	
		An experimental flocker integration supports persistent volumes that are not local to one node.

	The second provides an abstraction for a storage resource request (e.g. 8 Gb), which can be fulfilled with different storage backends.	
	Modifying the storage resource used by the Docker daemon on a cluster node requires temporarily removing the node from the cluster	
Networking	The networking model lets any pod can communicate with other pods and with any service.	Marathon's docker integration facilitates mapping container ports to host ports, which are a limited resource.
	The model requires two networks (one for pods, the other for services)	A container does not get its own IP by default, but it can if Mesos is integrated with Calico. Even so, multiple containers cannot share a network namespace (i.e. cannot talk to one another on localhost).
	Neither network is assumed to be (or needs to be) reachable from outside the cluster.	
	The most common way of meeting this requirement is to deploy an overlay network on the cluster nodes.	
Service Discovery	Pods discover services using intra-cluster DNS	Containers can discover services using DNS or reverse proxy.

Performance and scalability	With the release of 1.2, Kubernetes now supports 1000-node clusters. Kubernetes scalability is benchmarked against the following Service Level Objectives (SLOs):	Mesos has been simulated to scale to 50,000 nodes, although it is not clear how far scale has been pushed in production environments. Mesos can run LXC or Docker containers directly from the Marathon framework or it can fire up Kubernetes or Docker Swarm (the Docker-branded container manager) and let them do it.
	API responsiveness: 99% of all API calls return in less than 1s	
	Pod startup time: 99% of pods and their containers (with pre-pulled images) start within 5s.	

When should you use microservices

The single most important step on the path to a solid, workable approach to microservices is simply understanding the domain you're working in. If you can't understand it, or if you're still trying to figure it out, microservices could do more harm than good. But if you have a deep understanding, then you know where the boundaries are, what the dependencies are, so a microservices approach could be the right move.

Another important thing to have a handle on is your workflows – specifically how they might relate to the idea of a Distributed Transaction. If you know the paths each category of request will make through your system, and you understand where, how, and why each of those paths might fail, you could start to build out a distributed model of handling your requests.

Alongside understanding your workflows is monitoring your workflows. Monitoring is a subject greater than just "Microservice VS Monolith", but it should be something at the core of your engineering efforts. You may need a lot of data at your fingertips about various parts of your systems to understand why one of them is underperforming, or even throwing errors. If you have a solid approach for monitoring the various pieces of your system, you can begin to understand your systems behaviors as you increase its footprint horizontally.

And finally, when you can actually demonstrate value to your engineering organization, and the business as well, that moving to microservices will help you grow, scale, and make money. Although it's fun to build things and try new ideas out, at the end of the day the most important thing for many companies is their bottom line. If you have to delay putting out a new feature that will make the company revenue because a blogpost told you monoliths were "doing it wrong", you're going to need to justify that to the business. Sometimes these tradeoffs are worth it. Sometimes they aren't. Knowing how to pick your battles and spend time on the right technical debt will earn you a lot of credit in the long run.

Source:
https://opensource.com/resources/what-are-microservices
https://platform9.com/blog/compare-kubernetes-vs-docker-swarm

PKI (public key infrastructure)

A public key infrastructure (PKI) supports the distribution and identification of public encryption keys, enabling users and computers to both securely exchange data over networks such as the Internet and verify the identity of the other party.

Public key encryption, also called asymmetric encryption, is popular because it is more secure than secret key (symmetric) encryption. Two mathematically related keys, a public key and a private key, work together, with one used for encrypting and the other for decrypting (which one is used for which purpose depends on whether your goal is confidentiality of the data or authentication of the sender). The public key is made known to everyone who wants to engage in encrypted communications with the owner of the key pair. The private key never has to be shared with anyone; it is known only to its owner. This makes for a more secure system than the secret key method in which the same key is used for encrypting and decrypting and thus must be shared between the two communicating parties.

The problem with public key encryption is the difficulty of knowing whether a public key is really owned by the person it is claimed to belong to. A user could advertise that a public key belongs to Velabhai Bhedaru when in fact it doesn't; that user could then intercept messages intended for Velabhai Bhedaru and decrypt them with the private key belonging to the key pair. Thus, a method was needed for verifying the identity of the holder of key pairs.

That's where digital certificates come in. A trusted third party, called a certification authority, issues a certificate associated with a key pair to a user (or computer) whose identity it has already verified. Then other users and computers can rely on the veracity of the key holder's identity. This works somewhat like the issuance of identification cards by governmental entities or employers. The issuer has already checked out the identity of the person to whom the card is issued, so others (for example, stores to which the card holder writes checks) depend on the issuer's certification that the card holder is really whomever he/she claims to be.

Digital certificates contain information about the holder, the holder's public key, an expiration date, and the digital signature of the issuer (the certification authority). Managing digital certificates and their associated keys is complex, so the PKI was created to provide a framework for the issuance, renewal, revocation and management of certificates. Industry standard PKIs and their certificates are built on the X.509 specifications of the ISO.

The PKI environment is made up of five components:
Certification Authority (CA) -- serves as the root of trust that authenticates the identity of individuals, computers and other entities in the network.
Registration Authority (RA) -- is certified by a root CA to issue certificates for uses permitted by the CA. In a Microsoft PKI environment, the RA is normally called a subordinate CA.
Certificate Database -- saves certificate requests issued and revoked certificates from the RA or CA.
Certificate Store -- saves issued certificates and pending or rejected certificate requests from the local computer.
Key Archival Server -- saves encrypted private keys in a certificate database for disaster recovery purposes in case the Certificate Database is lost.

Issuance, Management and Revocation of Certificates

The process involved in issuing and managing certificates is complex. When a request for a certificate is made to a CA, a key pair must be created and signed by the requestor, then the public key is sent to the CA. The CA must verify the signature and identity based on its policies. When this is done, the CA signs the user's public key with the CA's private key. This creates the certificate, which is then sent back to the requestor. The certificate can then be published. Certificates can be issued for a number of different uses, including smart cards, IPSec, EFS, logon authentication, web authentication, email, and more.

Certificates are generally stored on the requestor's computer, but they can be moved (exported) to another computer. You also can export the certificate to back it up, and then import it to restore it.

There are many reasons a certificate might need to be revoked. If the key is compromised or the user leaves the organization, you'll want to revoke the certificate(s). In other words, you don't want other users, computers and applications to rely on that certificate anymore, so you must make it known to them that the certificate is no longer good. This is done by publishing and distributing a Certificate Revocation List (CRL). You can think of this as similar to the list of revoked credit cards that credit card companies distributed to merchants in the past. When you presented a credit card for payment, the merchant would check your card against the list to make certain it hadn't been revoked. Now the process is usually computerized; the card number is entered and the computer checks it against a database of revoked cards that is updated automatically.

Data Transmission:

The client and server can encrypt and decrypt all transmitted data with the symmetric session key generated during SSL handshake. TLS 1.2 protocol can be used to support this secure data transmission. This allows for a secure channel because only the client and the server know the symmetric session key, and the session key is only used for that session. If client want to connect to the same server the next day (session key expiry), a new session key would be created.

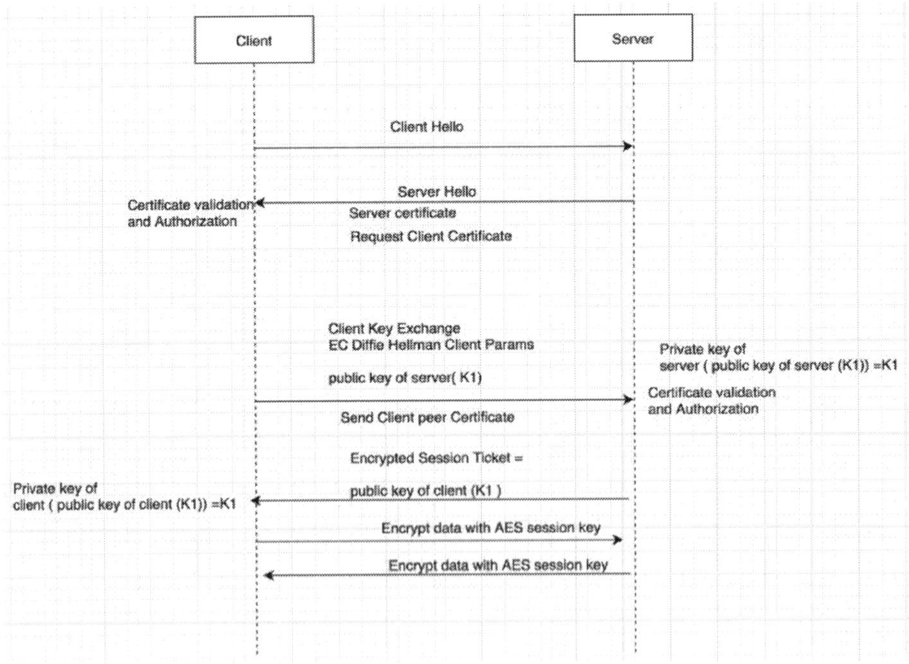

Tomcat Web Server

Apache Tomcat, known as “Tomcat” is an open-source web server that started as a servlet reference in 1999 and is developed and maintained by the Apache Software Foundation. It is a Java implementation that runs Java Servlets and JavaServer Pages, known as JSPs, as specified from Oracle.

Tomcat will serve any static content from a WAR file using The Deafult Servlet. This works great for serving files that are bundled with your Java code inside of a WAR file – it’s fast enough for most purposes and it just works, but with one major drawback: you have to re-deploy the WAR file it you want to add or amend a static file. That may work for you but if you are working in a development process where releasing new versions of your app requires sign-offs and rounds of testing then it doesn’t make sense to go through that process just to update a single image file because someone wants a slightly darker blue background on the contact page.

Tomcat provides flexibility to read files from anywhere on disk and serve them on a specific URL. This configuration is completely separate to your application config – you could, if you wanted, just start Tomcat and have it serve static files from disk with no webapps running. The configuration is in Tomcat’s server.xml configuration file and looks like this:

```
<Host appBase="webapps"   autoDeploy="false" name="localhost"
unpackWARs="true"
        xmlNamespaceAware="false" xmlValidation="false">   ...
   <Context docBase="/home/stuff" path="/static" />
</Host>
```

In HTTP 1.1, all connections between the browser and the server are considered persistent unless declared otherwise. Persistence, in this context, means to use a single TCP connection to send and receive multiple HTTP requests/responses, as opposed to opening a new connection for every single request/response pair.

In tomcat, the default HTTP connector is blocking and follows a one thread per connection model. This means that in order to serve 100 concurrent users, it requires 100 active threads. We end up wasting resources (the thread) because connections may not be used heavily, but just enough to avoid a timeout.

Opposed to this is the relatively new NIO or non-blocking connector. This connector has a couple of polling threads used to keep the connection alive for all connected users while worker threads are called whenever data (a new HTTP request) is available. This model leads to a much better sharing of resources (threads) and a larger number of concurrent users can be served from the same server.

In order to configure tomcat to use the Non-blocking NIO connector instead of the default blocking BIO one simply change the value of the protocol attribute of the connector tag in the server.xml
from HTTP/1.1 to org.apache.coyote.http11.Http11NioProtocol

```
<Connector connectionTimeout="20000" maxThreads="1000"
port="8080" protocol="org.apache.coyote.http11.Http11NioProtocol"
redirectPort="8443"/>
```

NGINX Server

Many Apache Tomcat deployments use the Apache HTTP Server for application delivery. Apache HTTP Server's thread-per-connection architecture delivers acceptable performance under low to medium load, but under heavy load the limitations of the architecture begin to surface. In one common scenario, the thread pool becomes exhausted when there is a large number of concurrent connections, which in turn delays acceptance of new connections until the threads are released. Issues like this, along with the small number of load-balancing configuration options in HTTP Server, limit its usefulness as a load balancer in high-traffic Apache Tomcat application server deployments.

NGINX and NGINX Plus eliminate HTTP Server's performance limitations by using asynchronous operations to achieve high concurrency without the overhead of threads. This architecture enables them to scale and handle a large number of simultaneous connections using a very small memory footprint. In addition to performance and scale, NGINX provides a number of benefits for Apache Tomcat applications:

Event driven Architecture - NGINX provides much greater scalability and resilience to traffic spikes and DOS attacks than WebLogic Server offers on its own.
HTTP/2 Support– NGINX supports the HTTP/2 protocol, which offers improved performance over HTTP/1.1.
LOAD BALANCING– The variety of load balancing algorithms in NGINX enable you to scale out your Tomcat applications as well as maintain high availability.
SSL/TLS Termination– NGINX can terminate SSL/TLS connections to offload that work from Tomcat application servers.
Caching- NGINX acts as a highly capable cache for both static and dynamic content, which greatly improves application performance.

And NGINX Plus, the enhanced and commercially supported product, builds on NGINX with additional enterprise-ready features:

Application health checks – NGINX Plus proactively monitors Tomcat application servers and stops sending requests to unhealthy servers.

Session persistence – NGINX Plus leverages the JSESSIONID cookie to ensure that a user's requests are forwarded to the same Tomcat application server every time.
On-the-fly reconfiguration of load-balanced servers – You can reconfigure load-balanced server groups on the fly using the Domain Name System (DNS) or a simple HTTP API.
Live activity monitoring – NGINX Plus has a real-time activity monitoring interface that provides key load and performance metrics.

Made in the USA
Monee, IL
04 November 2026

67386097R10050